PEOPLES
of
EASTERN ASIA

Indonesia

PEOPLES
of
EASTERN ASIA

Volume 5
Indonesia

MARSHALL CAVENDISH
NEW YORK • LONDON • SINGAPORE

Marshall Cavendish Corporation
99 White Plains Road
Tarrytown, New York 10591
www.marshallcavendish.com

©2005 Marshall Cavendish Corporation

All rights reserved. No part of this book may be reproduced or utilized in any form or by any means, electronic or mechanical, including photocopying, recording, or by any information storage and retrieval system, without prior written permission from the publisher and the copyright holders.

Consultants:
   Emily K. Bloch, Department of South Asian Languages
      and Civilizations, University of Chicago
   Amy Rossabi, MA in Southeast Asian History
   Morris Rossabi, Professor and Senior Research Scholar,
      Columbia University

Contributing authors:
   Fiona Macdonald
   Gillian Stacey
   Philip Steele

Marshall Cavendish
   Editor: Marian Armstrong
   Editorial Director: Paul Bernabeo
   Production Manager: Michael Esposito

Discovery Books
   Managing Editor: Paul Humphrey
   Project Editor: Kate Taylor
   Design Concept: Ian Winton
   Designer: Barry Dwyer
   Cartographer: Stefan Chabluk
   Picture Researcher: Laura Durman

The publishers would like to thank the following for their permission to reproduce photographs:
   akg-images: 236, 239, 240 (Erich Lessing: 237); Axiom (C. Bowman: 281; Jim Holmes: 248; Martin Stolworthy: 250 bottom; George Wright: 270); CORBIS: 279 (Tiziana & Gianni Baldizzone: 266; Morton Beebe: 274; Dean Conger: 276 bottom; Sergio Dorantes: 255; Lindsay Hebberd: 235; Jeremy Horner: 231; Dave G. Houser: 257; Wolfgang Kaehler: 265, 282; Jufri Kemal: 244; Charles O'Rear: 254; Michael S. Yamashita: 268; Jim Zuckerman: 269); Hutchison: 249 (Robert Francis: 252; Jeremy Horner: 262, 276 top; P. W. Rippon: 253); Panos (Peter Barker: 277; J. C. Callow: 261; Jean-Léo Dugast: 263; Jeremy Hartley: 246, 283; Chris Stowers: 242, 243, 260 bottom; D. Tatlow: 259); David Simson – DASPHOTOGB@aol.com: 278; Still Pictures (Alain Compost: Mark Edwards: 256; Ron Giling: 272; Paul Harrison: 234, 245, 258; 260 top; Thomas Kelly: cover; Dario Novellino: 250 top, 271); Trip (R. Belbin: 280; T. Bognar: 233; D. Clegg: 247, 273; J. Sweeney: 264)

(cover) A Tibetan woman with her child strapped to her back.

Editor's note: Many systems of dating have been used by different cultures throughout history. *Peoples of Eastern Asia* uses B.C.E. (Before Common Era) and C.E. (Common Era) instead of B.C. (Before Christ) and A.D. (Anno Domini, "In the Year of the Lord").

Library of Congress Cataloging-in-Publication Data

Peoples of Eastern Asia.
      p. cm.
   Includes bibliographical references and index.
   Contents: v. 1. Bangladesh-Brunei -- v. 2. Cambodia-China -- v. 3. China-East Timor -- v. 4. India -- v. 5. Indonesia -- v. 6. Japan-Korea, North -- v. 7. Korea, South-Malaysia -- v. 8. Mongolia-Nepal -- v. 9. Philippines-Sri Lanka -- v. 10. Taiwan-Vietnam.
   ISBN 0-7614-7547-8 (set : alk. paper) -- ISBN 0-7614-7548-6 (v. 1 : alk. paper) -- ISBN 0-7614-7549-4 (v. 2 : alk. paper) -- ISBN 0-7614-7550-8 (v. 3 : alk. paper) -- ISBN 0-7614-7551-6 (v. 4 : alk. paper) -- ISBN 0-7614-7552-4 (v. 5 : alk. paper) -- ISBN 0-7614-7553-2 (v. 6 : alk. paper) -- ISBN 0-7614-7554-0 (v. 7 : alk. paper) -- ISBN 0-7614-7555-9 (v. 8 : alk. paper) -- ISBN 0-7614-7556-7 (v. 9 : alk. paper) -- ISBN 0-7614-7557-5 (v. 10 : alk. paper) -- ISBN 0-7614-7558-3 (v. 11 : index vol. : alk. paper)
   1. East Asia. 2. Asia, Southeastern. 3. South Asia. 4. Ethnology--East Asia. 5. Ethnology--Asia, Southeastern. 6. Ethnology--South Asia.

DS511.P457 2004
950--dc22

2003069645

   ISBN 0-7614-7547-8 (set : alk. paper)
   ISBN 0-7614-7552-4 (v. 5 : alk. paper)

Printed in China
09 08 07 06 05 04   6 5 4 3 2 1

Contents

INDONESIA

INDONESIA IS A COUNTRY IN SOUTHEAST ASIA. It consists of five large islands and approximately seventeen thousand smaller ones.

Indonesia is the world's largest archipelago. It covers a vast area — more than 779,000 square miles (2,019,000 square kilometers). Less than half of its islands are inhabited.

Indonesia's numerous small islands are low lying. Its larger islands are more mountainous, with more than seventy active volcanoes. The highest mountain, on Irian Jaya, is Puncak

Jaya and stands at 16,535 feet (5,040 meters). Although it lies close to the equator, this peak remains snow covered all year-round. There are areas of flat land in river valleys and along many coasts. Some islands, especially Bali, have beautiful beaches with coral reefs. Other beaches are sticky with volcanic mud and tangled mangrove swamps.

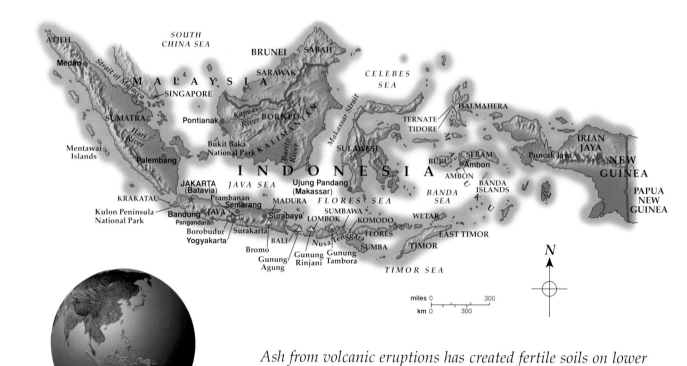

Ash from volcanic eruptions has created fertile soils on lower mountain slopes. Tropical rain forests grow there, providing a home to thousands of rare animals, birds, insects, and plants, but in recent years, mining, agribusiness, and illegal logging have devastated Indonesia's forests, and many species are now in danger.

A sandy beach on the island of Flores, in the Nusa Tenggara region. There are around seventeen thousand islands in the Indonesian archipelago.

make stone tools and weapons, light fires, and build simple shelters of twigs and leaves. Later they learned how to grow rice, weave cloth, and make valuable objects, such as drums and bells, from the migrants who arrived from Vietnam and China between 3000 and 700 B.C.E., bringing with them many technological skills. Soon they

FACTS AND FIGURES

Official name: *Republic of Indonesia*

Status: *Independent state*

Capital: *Jakarta*

Major towns: *Surabaya, Bandung, Medan, Semarang, Yogyakarta*

Area: *779,675 square miles (2,019,358 square kilometers)*

Population: *231,328,000*

Population density: *297 per square mile (115 per square kilometer)*

Peoples: *45 percent Javanese; 14 percent Sundanese; 7.5 percent Madurese; 7.5 percent coastal Malay; 26 percent others, mostly Melanesians, Chinese, Papuans, Arabs, Indians, Australians, and Portuguese*

Official language: *Bahasa Indonesia*

Currency: *Indonesian rupiah (IDR)*

National day: *Independence Day (August 17)*

Country's name: *Indonesia is locally known as* Tanah Air Kita, *meaning "Our earth and water."*

The First Indonesians

Humans and their ancestors have lived in Indonesia (ihn-doe-NEEZ-yah) for almost a million years. In 1890 archaeologists discovered the remains of a skull belonging to an early human, known as *Homo erectus*, on the island of Java (JAH-vuh). It was over 800,000 years old. Modern humans, like ourselves, arrived in Indonesia much later, around 40,000 B.C.E. They traveled from Myanmar (formerly Burma: see MYANMAR), Thailand, and the Philippines, walking across "land bridges"—stretches of the seabed left uncovered when the oceans froze during past Ice Ages.

These modern humans lived by hunting wild animals, fishing, and gathering wild fruits, nuts, and seeds. They knew how to

Time line:	Modern humans arrive in Indonesia	Migrants from China and Vietnam arrive; bring new metalworking and rice-growing skills
	40,000 B.C.E.	**3000–700 B.C.E.**

CLIMATE

Indonesia has an equatorial climate and is hot and humid year-round. There is a dry season from June to October and a rainy season, with frequent thunderstorms and monsoon winds, from November to March. Temperatures are lowest in the high mountains and highest along the coast.

	Jakarta	Sumatra	Kalimantan	Maluku
Average January temperature:	78°F (26°C)	81°F (27°C)	79°F (26°C)	82°F (28°C)
Average July temperature:	79°F (26°C)	81°F (27°C)	77°F (25°C)	77°F (25°C)
Average annual precipitation:	72 in. (183 cm)	164 in. (417 cm)	88 in. (224 cm)	136 in. (345 cm)

settled down and began to build villages instead of roaming over the countryside.

Growing rice in flooded paddies produced excellent crops year-round, but growing rice required large numbers of workers and someone to organize them. Village leaders probably met together to decide how to make the best use of the local rice fields. Over the centuries certain villages and families became more powerful than others. By around 100 C.E. members of these families were respected and obeyed as local chiefs and even as kings.

Around the same time merchants from China and many other Southeast Asian lands sailed to Indonesia to trade. They wanted to buy local produce—especially gold, spices, sandalwood, and sweet-smelling resin (plant gum). In this way Indonesians came into contact with many different peoples, including Hindus from India. Many Indonesians soon became Hindus. By about 400 there were Hindu kingdoms on many Indonesian islands.

There were also many Buddhist monks who arrived from India. They were probably invited, as expert scholars, by Indonesian Hindu kings.

Early Empires

By around 600 one Indonesian kingdom had become much more powerful than the rest. Based in Palembang (pael-uhm-BANG) in Sumatra (soo-MAH-truh), it was ruled by the Srivijaya (sree-wih-JAW-yuh) dynasty of kings. They were Hindus, but they also encouraged Buddhists to live and work in their lands. Their power stretched from Thailand to west Kalimantan (ka-lih-MAHN-tuhn), and their wealth came from taxing trade in valuable Indonesian goods (including spices, turtle shells, and precious stones), demanding tribute from conquered peoples, and controlling ships sailing through the Strait of Malacca (muh-LAH-kuh)—an important seaway leading from the Indian Ocean to the South China Sea.

Small states ruled by local chiefs trade with merchants from China	Small Hindu kingdoms become powerful; invite Buddhist monks to settle	Srivijaya kings rule large empire from their base in Sumatra
100 C.E.	**400**	**600–1300**

Under Srivijaya rule Palembang became a great center of religious learning. Over a thousand Buddhist monks lived there.

The Srivijaya empire controlled a vast area of sea together with many settlements around the Indonesian coast, but its power did not stretch far inland. By around 700 rival land-based empires developed in central Java. They were ruled by the Sailendra (sie-LEHN-druh) kings, who were Buddhists, and the Mataram (MAH-tuh-ruhm), or Sanjaya, kings, who were Hindus. Their wealth came from the fertile rice fields of Java and from the very large numbers of people who lived there. Sailendra and Mataram kings organized their people into massive work teams and employed them to build magnificent temples and palaces. The most famous Buddhist temple is at Borobudur (boer-uh-buh-DUHR); the best Hindu monuments are at Prambanan (pruhm-BAE-nuhn), both in Java. Over thirty temples and palaces still survive there, including the Prambanan Complex — a cluster of three huge temples surrounded by 224 smaller ones, plus many beautiful statues.

Sailendra and Mataram kings were tolerant of each other's faiths. They also allowed ordinary people to continue with their ancient animist beliefs (that all living things, and many mountains, trees, and streams, have spirits). Over the years all three faiths blended together with local craft traditions and skills to create a distinctive Javanese culture.

However, the Sailendra and Mataram dynasties also spent many years fighting each other. Because

of this, after around 1000 their power began to decline. New, stronger kingdoms grew up in eastern Java and took over their lands. The greatest of these was the Hindu Majapahit (mah-huh-PAH-hiht) empire, founded in 1292. Over the next two hundred years Majapahit troops conquered a vast area, including lands in Sumatra, Bali (BAHL-ee), Sulawesi (soo-lah-WAE-see), Kalimantan, and Timor (TEE-moer). Majapahit kings made friendly alliances with many other powerful rulers in China, Vietnam, and other parts of Southeast Asia and encouraged learning and all the arts, but between 1400 and 1600 the empire's power slowly collapsed as Majapahit kings failed to control all their far-flung territories

Part of the temple complex at Prambanan, Java, built for the Mataram dynasty between 832 and 856 C.E. The three temples are dedicated to the Hindu gods Shiva, Vishnu, and Brahma.

First Muslims arrive in western Indonesia	Sailendra (Buddhist) and Mataram (Hindu) kings rule powerful states in Java	Borobudur temple built
700	**700–1000**	**ca. 750**

and struggled against rebels in their homeland of Java.

In Sumatra the mighty Srivijaya empire was also beginning to weaken. From around 1100 it was attacked by sailors from the Chola (CHOE-luh) kingdom in southern India. By 1300 Srivijaya rulers could no longer keep control of their lands, and the empire split into many smaller states. Control of shipping in the Strait of Malacca passed to a new kingdom called Melaka (muh-LUH-ca) on the Malay (muh-LAE) Peninsula. This new kingdom soon grew strong enough to take over many lands that Srivijaya once ruled.

Borobudur

The Buddhist temple of Borobudur, on the Indonesian island of Java, is one of Asia's great historic monuments. It was built between 750 and 785 C.E. by the Sailendra dynasty, who ruled Java. Its construction used over 2,000,000 cubic feet (56,000 cubic meters) of stone.

Borobudur is shaped like a massive stupa (Buddhist burial mound) balanced on top of nine terraces, which are supported by a huge base measuring 1,270 square feet (118 square meters). The whole temple is covered with wonderful carvings, which show the entire universe, from humans and animals at the bottom to nirvana (the blissful end of life, according to Buddhist beliefs) at the top. There are also over four hundred images of the Buddha.

Borobudur was abandoned around 1000 C.E. and neglected for around nine hundred years. It was repaired between 1973 and 1983 at a cost of $25 million. Today it is visited by millions of tourists every year.

A statue of the Buddha gazes out over seventy-two small stupas (dome-shaped mounds) that form part of the great Buddhist temple at Borobudur, Java.

The Spread of Islam

Like Hinduism and Buddhism, the faith of Islam was brought to Indonesia by traders. They traveled from Arabia and northwest India, stopping in Sumatra on their long voyages to and from China. After around 700 they set up small coastal settlements in

Chola kings from India attack Indonesian kingdoms	Majapahit kings from Java rule empire stretching to Timor	Islam becomes official religion in most of Indonesia; sailors from Makassar reach Australia
1100	**1292–ca. 1500**	**ca. 1450**

northern Sumatra. During the next four hundred years the Muslim faith slowly spread eastward to other Indonesian islands. Around 1450 Majapahit kings made Islam the official religion of their empire. When the empire lands were split up into many smaller kingdoms, the new rulers made Islam their state religion too.

While the Majapahit empire was collapsing, new Muslim states were winning power elsewhere in Indonesia. They were based in trading cities on the north coast of Java and in Makassar (muh-KAS-suh) on the island of Sulawesi. Sailors from Makassar (present-day Ujung Pandang) made regular trading voyages to New Guinea and even to northern Australia—the first Indonesian merchants to venture that far.

Europeans Arrive

The Indian and Arab traders who visited Indonesia to buy resins and spices sold them at high prices to eager customers throughout Europe and the Middle East. Travelers, including the famous Italian explorer Marco Polo, also described the mysterious Indonesian Spice Islands in popular books. It is therefore not surprising that some enterprising European merchants wanted to go to Indonesia

The Spice Islands

Until around 1750, two small Indonesian islands, Ternate (ter-NAET-ee) and Tidore (tih-DOER-ee) in the north Maluku (muh-LUH-ca) region, were the world's main producers of nutmegs — the large seeds of the pala *(PAH-luh) tree — and cloves — the dried flower buds of the* cengkeh *(SAENG-kuh) tree. In the past, both were widely used to flavor foods. Cloves were also used to soothe toothaches. Both spices are still used in cakes and puddings; cloves also flavor toothpaste and chewing gum. Until the so-called Spice Islands were conquered by Portugal in 1512, Arab and Indian merchants traveled vast distances to buy cloves and nutmegs on the islands. They carried them back to eager customers in Europe and the Middle East, where they sold for high prices. A single shipload of dried cloves could make a merchant rich for life!*

The fruit of the pala tree. The nutmeg is in the center. It is surrounded by a reddish lacy covering, which is dried and used as a spice, called mace.

First Europeans (Portuguese) arrive	First Dutch soldiers arrive	Dutch control many Indonesian islands and all of the spice trade
1512	**1596**	**1700**

themselves, but the voyage to Southeast Asia from Europe was long and dangerous. Until 1498 few thought that it could be done. Then, that year, Portuguese explorer Vasco da Gama sailed from Europe, around the southern tip of Africa, to the west coast of India. Just a few years later, in 1512, the first Portuguese sailors reached the Strait of Malacca and sighted the islands of Indonesia. They captured Maluku, the center of the Indonesian spice trade, and set up fortified trading settlements on several other Indonesian islands.

Before long other European traders also sailed to Indonesia, from Britain, Spain, and, especially, the Netherlands. The first Dutch arrived in 1596. They lost a ship and many men but returned home with a rich cargo of spices. To encourage further trade, in 1602 the government of the Netherlands joined all Dutch merchants with an interest in Southeast Asia into a single business organization. Named the Dutch East India Company, it was given a monopoly (sole rights) to trade with Indonesia. Dutch merchants, and the Dutch government, hoped to win complete control of the Indonesian spice trade, using violence if necessary.

The campaign in Indonesia was led by Jan Pieterszoon

Coen. He commanded a fleet of armed ships carrying soldiers ready to fight against other Europeans in Indonesia and against local Indonesian rulers. In 1603 the Dutch massacred two-thirds of the local people as they fought to gain control of the Banda (BAWN-duh) Islands. They went on to defeat the Portuguese in Maluku in 1605 and eventually, in 1610, won permission from the ruler of Jakarta (juh-KAHR-tuh), in Java, to build a trading post there. Over the next few years the Dutch soldiers turned it into a fort. They battled against English merchants and the local Indonesian people. In 1619 they destroyed the old Indonesian city and built themselves a new town on the site. They called it Batavia (buh-TAE-vee-uh) after a region of the Netherlands. It became the center of Dutch power in Indonesia.

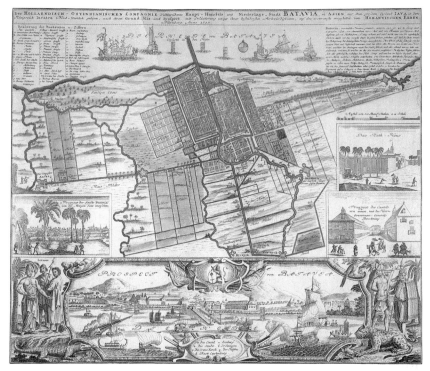

The Dutch city of Batavia, in Java, in 1733. It was built like a European city, with streets and houses arranged in a squared grid pattern.

Dutch East India Company closed down because of corruption	War between Dutch and English in Indonesia	The Paderi War, rebels in Sumatra fight Dutch
1799	**1811**	**1821**

Dutch East India Company Rules

From their base in Batavia (present day Jakarta) the Dutch continued to take over more Indonesian land and to drive other Europeans out of Indonesian territory. They encouraged wars between rival Indonesian rulers so that they would become weak and easier to attack. These wars caused tremendous suffering among ordinary Indonesian people and badly damaged their homes and fields.

By 1700 the Dutch East India Company controlled all of the Indonesian spice trade and many Indonesian kingdoms. Their triumph did not last long. In 1780 they were forced to end their monopoly as part of a treaty between Britain and the Netherlands made at the end of wars fought far away from Indonesia, on land

Ships belonging to the Dutch East India Company, 1657. They had wide, deep hulls to carry valuable cargoes of spices and huge sails to catch the wind.

and at sea in Europe. The Company itself also faced serious problems. Its officials were fierce fighters, but they were not good businessmen. Nor were they all honest. Dutch government investigators found evidence of widespread smuggling and corruption, as well as massive debts. In 1799 the Dutch government closed the Company down and took over all its lands. They became part of a new Dutch empire in Africa and Asia.

Dutch Empire

Governors of the new Dutch empire in Indonesia soon discovered that they were not welcome there. They faced opposition from local people and attacks by British

Start of rebellion against Dutch on Java led by Prince Diponegoro	Dutch introduce Cultivation System and develop large, one-crop plantations
1825	**1830**

troops. British soldiers led by Sir Thomas Stamford Raffles captured the Dutch capital of Batavia in 1811. Raffles occupied the city for six years before he was forced to retreat. A more serious threat to Dutch rule came in 1821 when three Islamic holy men in Sumatra led Indonesian soldiers to fight against the Dutch in the Paderi (PAH-dree) War, which lasted until 1837. Meanwhile, in 1825, Javanese Prince Diponegoro led local people in a rebellion against Dutch rule. This caused tremendous suffering in Java and over 200,000 Javanese civilians died, mostly from starvation, as fighting disrupted farming and wrecked the paddies where rice was grown.

Colonial Rule

After Diponegoro was defeated in 1830, the Dutch took steps to tighten their control of Indonesia. They introduced a new kind of farming, called the Cultivation System, which was designed to bring ordinary Indonesian people, especially in Java, under close Dutch supervision and make money for the Dutch rulers at the same time. Under the Cultivation System farmers had to give up almost half of their land to grow crops, mostly indigo (used to dye cloth), coffee, and sugar, for their Dutch masters. This was sent back to Europe. The Dutch made a great deal of money from this trade, but many poor Indonesian farmers no longer had enough land to feed themselves, and many families starved.

In 1870 the Dutch introduced a new money-making scheme called the Liberal System. This allowed foreigners to rent large estates in Indonesia from the Dutch colonial rulers. The Dutch believed that these foreign private companies would farm more efficiently, improve the quality of crops, and encourage the local economy to grow, thereby helping all Indonesians, rich and poor. This did not happen, partly because of changes in world trading conditions and partly because Indonesian coffee and sugar plantations (large estates, where only single crops were planted) were hit by serious outbreaks of plant disease.

In the late nineteenth century the Dutch introduced new, more humane policies toward Indonesian people. They built roads, flood barriers, and irrigation systems to help local farmers. Hospitals and schools were built to help Indonesian families, but the Dutch continued to treat Indonesian people as second-class citizens.

Nationalist Protests

Throughout the period of colonial rule the Dutch faced repeated attacks from Indonesian rulers and their armies, who wanted the right to rule their own homeland. The Balinese fought for over sixty years (1846–1908) before surrendering to the Dutch, while the people of Atjeh (AH-cheh), in northern Sumatra, fought a war that lasted intermittently from 1873 to 1942. Lombok (LAWM-bawk) only agreed to accept Dutch rule in 1894 and Sulawesi in 1905. Irian Jaya remained independent until 1920. There were also new, nationalist movements such as Sarekat Islam (the Islamic Association), founded in 1909; the PKI (Perserikatan Kommunist Indonesia:

Dutch introduce new Liberal System and foreign companies take control of Indonesian land	Sarekat Islam (Islamic Association) founded to fight for independence	Planned Communist revolution fails
1870	**1909**	**1926**

Not all Indonesians welcomed the Japanese. These Indonesian soldiers fought alongside Dutch colonial troops against Japanese invaders in 1942.

Indonesian Communist Party), which tried to organize a revolution in 1926; and the PNI (Partai Nasional Indonesia), founded in 1927. The PNI, in particular, won mass support among ordinary Indonesian people. Frightened of its power, the Dutch sent its leader, Achmed Sukarno, to jail along with many other nationalist campaigners.

World War and After

In 1940 German troops invaded the Netherlands, and the Dutch government was forced to flee. Two years later the Japanese invaded Indonesia. They were keen to get control of Indonesia's rich resources of oil, rubber, and bauxite (a mineral ore used to produce aluminum, which was used in making warplanes). At first most Indonesians welcomed the Japanese. They hoped Japanese soldiers would help them end Dutch colonial rule. Many Japanese, including powerful Admiral Maeda, supported their aims. The Japanese also encouraged revolutionary youth groups who campaigned for independence on many Indonesian islands.

The Japanese eventually lost the war, but Admiral Maeda was determined to do all

Partai Nasional Indonesia (Indonesian National Party) founded; its leader, Achmed Sukarno, put in prison	Japanese invade and occupy Indonesia; they support independence campaigners
1927	**1942**

Indonesian independence leader Achmed Sukarno (center, in black hat), surrounded by supporters, listening to speeches at an election rally in 1955.

and appointed himself president, with fellow-campaigner Dr. Hatta as his deputy.

The Dutch and their allies did not agree with Sukarno's plans. British troops arrived in Indonesia in 1945 to accept the Japanese surrender and declared that the Japanese had no power to grant independence to Indonesia. For a few months the British fought fiercely against Indonesian soldiers, then withdrew in 1946, as soon as a large Dutch army arrived. Fighting between the Dutch and Indonesian independence campaigners continued for the next three years until the Dutch were forced by international opinion to give Indonesians their independence in December 1949. The next year Indonesia joined the United Nations—a sign that it was recognized by the whole international community.

A New Nation

The new nation of Indonesia was not an easy country to rule. It was vast, with poor communications, and many natural obstacles, such as seasonal floods, earthquakes, and volcanoes. Local farms and businesses were small and undeveloped, and there was hardly any industry. Many towns, cities, and harbors had been damaged during the Japanese occupation and in the fighting for independence. There were very few

he could to help the Indonesian independence campaigners before he handed over power. He sheltered PNI leader Achmed Sukarno from his enemies while he (Sukarno) drafted a Declaration of Independence. On August 17, 1945, just two days after the Japanese surrendered to Britain and its allies, Sukarno announced that the new nation of Indonesia had been born. He set up a provisional government

Sukarno declares new Indonesian nation is born, but Dutch refuse to accept this and fight	After pressure from international community, Indonesia finally becomes independent; Sukarno becomes president; declares policy of Pancasila
1945–1949	**1949**

doctors, nurses, scientists, or teachers. Most men and women could not read and write. The population was growing fast and needed food and housing. There were rival political parties and many separatist groups who wanted independence for their own islands or regions, for example, in Sumatra, Sulawesi, and west Java. The many different peoples of Indonesia had never been ruled as one nation before. Could the new government govern, and please, them all?

Most Indonesians greeted independence with great enthusiasm and were prepared to accept Sukarno's doctrine of *Pancasila* (puhn-KUH-see-luh), meaning "Five Principles" (faith in God, humanity, nationalism, representative government, and social justice), as the basis for their new state. However, many people accused him of betraying his ideals. In 1957 he introduced his own political system, which he called guided democracy. This system gave him enormous personal power. Unlike Western democracy, which is based on "one person, one vote," Sukarno's guided democracy was inspired by traditional village councils in Indonesia, where decisions were made by village chiefs after discussions with local people. Many Indonesians, especially top army officers, were also suspicious of Sukarno's close friendship with the Soviet Union, fearing that communists were planning to take over their land. Sukarno won praise for his campaign to drive the Dutch out of Irian Jaya (which he achieved in the 1960s), but he was widely criticized for trying to take over the independent states of Sabah,

Sarawak, and Brunei on the island of Borneo (BOR-nee-oe).

By the 1960s Sukarno was growing old and ill. His government also faced serious economic problems. In 1965 communists in Indonesia tried to seize power by kidnapping, then murdering, top army commanders. Some people accused Sukarno of secretly encouraging them. They claimed he wanted to remove powerful army leaders and at the same time have an excuse for punishing senior communists. If this is true, Sukarno's plan worked, but it had savage consequences. After the murders, a surviving army leader, Major General Suharto, took control of the country. In 1966, after several months of chaos, he eventually restored law and order. During that time almost half a million communist supporters were killed and thousands more were imprisoned without trial. Armed gangs terrorized the countryside, and many innocent people feared for their lives. Sukarno was removed from power (after the army staged another attempted coup), and Suharto was named acting president in 1967.

The New Order

Suharto was determined to rule in a very different way from Sukarno. He called his plans for Indonesia the New Order. They included economic reform, new commercial and political links with Western nations, and religious tolerance (except for animists and atheists). He encouraged new development, especially in big cities, and new industries and

Sukarno introduces new policy of guided democracy, giving himself great personal power	Communist party tries, but fails, to take over power; many communists killed as Sukarno allows reprisals
1957	**1965–1966**

Independent Indonesia became a staunchly Muslim state. This poster shows President Suharto (left) shaking hands with Muslim community leader Dr. Hatta.

technology. He also promoted international trade. After oil price rises in the 1970s brought new wealth to Indonesia, he built new hospitals and schools. He encouraged modern farming methods, increased crop production, and ended food shortages. The fear of famine in the countryside disappeared. His government built new roads, developed the tourist industry—especially on Bali—and encouraged modern communications,

though it liked to keep most media under strict government control.

However, there were less welcome changes. Suharto remained fiercely anti-communist. He also refused to let opposition parties freely express their views, forcing many of them to disband. Anyone who dared criticize his policies was put in jail; many were tortured and killed. There was widespread corruption, in government, business, and the civil service. Suharto himself became infamous for the lavish gifts and favors he gave to his own family. The gap between rich and poor increased. Profits from new, big enterprises were not spread fairly throughout the population. Most stayed in the hands of wealthy businesspeople who often had close connections with Suharto, his family, or his friends.

Suharto dealt harshly with rebels and separatist movements in remote parts of Indonesia. He caused an international outcry by invading the former Portuguese colony of East Timor as soon as it became independent in 1975. He also fought against independence campaigners in Irian Jaya.

Throughout the 1970s and 1980s Indonesia shared in the economic boom caused by the rapid development of high-tech and manufacturing businesses throughout Southeast Asia and around the Pacific Rim. This rise in prosperity kept Suharto in power until an economic crisis starting in Thailand led to his fall from

Sukarno replaced as president by Suharto; his New Order policy aims for economic reform and modernization, but there is widespread corruption	Boom years of economic growth, but restrictions on civil rights	Indonesia invades East Timor
1967	**1970s–1980s**	**1975**

power in 1998. Economies throughout Southeast Asia were severely shaken; Indonesia's faced complete ruin. Prices increased, inflation rose dangerously high, businesses collapsed, and many people lost their jobs. Suharto appealed to United Nations organizations, including the International Monetary Fund, for help. They agreed but demanded government reform. Many Indonesians also staged protests against corruption and human rights abuses. There were riots and looting in many big cities, much property was destroyed, and many people were killed for their beliefs. To prevent Indonesia from collapsing into chaos, Suharto was forced to resign in May 1998.

A panel of independent observers (seated at desks) monitors the progress of free, democratic elections organized by B. J. Habibie in 1999.

New Plans

Suharto was replaced as president by his friend and vice-president, B. J. Habibie. Following instructions from the International Monetary Fund, Habibie organized elections in June 1999. Several parties won a large share of the vote, but none was the outright winner, so the People's Consultative Assembly (made up of elected members of Parliament, plus two hundred respected appointees) chose Muslim scholar Abdurrahman Wahid as president, with Megawati Sukarnoputri (daughter of former president Sukarno) as his deputy. Together they made plans to restore democracy, remove corruption, and renew economic stability. It soon became clear, however, that Wahid lacked the political experience needed to be an

Economic crisis leads to mass riots; Suharto forced to hand over power	Free democratic elections; plans for end to corruption and economic renewal
1998	**1999**

Two Indonesian leaders with plans for reform. Megawati Sukarnoputri (left) replaced Abdurrahman Wahid (right) as president in 2001.

Land of Many Peoples

Indonesia is home to over three hundred different ethnic groups. In the past many of these communities were cut off from one another by Indonesia's mountainous terrain or by the sea. As a result they developed many different local customs and traditions, known as *adat* (uh-DAHT: traditional law), and numerous local dialects. Today all the different regions of Indonesia are linked by modern media, especially radio and television, and by the use of the national language, *Bahasa* (buh-HAH-suh) Indonesia. They all have to obey the same national laws. Even so, local communities still like to follow their own adat wherever possible and remain proud of their own local identity and heritage.

Most Indonesians are Malays and are closely related to peoples living elsewhere in Southeast Asia, especially in the neighboring nations of Malaysia and Brunei. The Javanese are the largest Malay group, making up around 45 percent of Indonesia's population. Other numerous Malay peoples include the Sundanese and the Madurese (mahj-uh-REES). Some Malay communities, like the Balinese, have a long tradition of contact with people from foreign countries. Others, such as the Dayak (DIE-ak), who live in remote inland regions of Kalimantan, and the Ngada (ehng-GAH-duh), who live on Flores (FLOER-ehz), have mostly been isolated from outsiders until the last hundred years.

Melanesian people, who are related to the inhabitants of Fiji (FEE-jee) and Vanuatu (vah-noo-AH-too), live on several eastern

effective president. In August 2000 he handed over day-to-day control of the government to Sukarnoputri. In 2001 fresh elections were held, and she was chosen as president.

Sukarnoputri has vowed to continue with her plans for economic and political reform, but many problems of corruption and financial weakness remain. There are also continuing tensions between central government and local separatist groups in several regions of Indonesia. In October 2002 a serious terrorist attack on the island of Bali threatened Indonesia's important tourist industry and increased international concerns about Indonesia's low level of security. There was also concern that Indonesia was being used as a base by terrorist organizations.

Megawati Sukarnoputri becomes president	Islamic terrorist attack on Bali and unrest in several provinces
2001	**2002**

Indonesian islands, including Irian Jaya and Timor. In the same region there are also many Papuans (puh-POO-uhnz)—the original inhabitants of Irian Jaya and the neighboring nation of Papua New Guinea.

The Chinese ethnic community is descended from traders, sailors, and laborers who came to work in Indonesia after around 1500. Today they are the most prosperous group in Indonesia, working as storekeepers, running hotels, and controlling multi-million dollar businesses, including factories and banks. They often face discrimination from other Indonesians, who are jealous of their wealth and success. The government also discriminates against them, using laws to discourage the use of Chinese words and names and banning other Indonesian citizens from learning Chinese.

Smaller minority groups include Arab and Indian families. Their ancestors were traders who visited Indonesia's rich Spice Islands from around 600 C.E. More recent arrivals include Australian expatriates, who work mainly in the mining and tourism industries, together with businesspeople, environmentalists, and aid agency workers from Australia, Europe, and the United States. They often come to live in Indonesia on short-term contracts that last from one to ten years.

Indonesia's population is big and growing fast. Indonesia is the fourth most populous nation in the world, and about one-third of its citizens are under fourteen. Within ten years most of them will be married and having children of their own. To try and halt the rapid population growth, which might lead to poverty, hunger, and disease, the Indonesian government sponsors family-planning programs, such as the "Dua Anak Cukup"

Children from Java. Their community recently benefited from a UNICEF aid project that helped members grow healthy green vegetables and raise goats.

(Two Children Are Enough) campaign. It also encourages poor families from densely populated islands, such as Java, to move to remote regions where fewer people live. This policy—known as *transmigrasi* (tranz-mee-GRA-see)—is not always successful. Incomers do not always understand local languages or traditions and may not have the farming skills to survive in the countryside. They are away from their families and friends and are sometimes resented, or even attacked, by "host" communities, who fear that they will take over their land.

Languages

Indonesia has one official language, Bahasa Indonesia (*Bahasa* means "language"). It is used for all official business, from debates in the House of Representatives (the national government assembly) to lessons in elementary schools. Belonging to the Malayo-Polynesian group of languages that are widely spoken throughout Southeast Asia, it is spoken by most Indonesians. They almost all speak another language as well. There are at least 365 local languages and dialects—some Malay, some Melanesian, and some Papuan. Educated people, and some older people, who remember colonial rule, also speak English or Dutch. Muslim scholars learn Arabic, and Indonesians of Chinese ancestry speak Chinese or a hybrid language based on a Chinese dialect mixed with Bahasa Indonesia.

Religious Beliefs

Indonesia is a very religious society. Belief in "One God" is compulsory by law, and religious observances and ceremonies play an important part in almost all Indonesian people's lives. Around 88 percent of Indonesian people are Muslims, making Indonesia the largest Muslim nation in the world. Nearly all Indonesians belong to the Sunni (SOON-ee) branch of Islam. They pray five times daily; in cities and towns there are prayer rooms attached to many public buildings, such as railroad stations. They fast

Women and young children in front of government family-planning signs. Indonesian population planners advise that families should have no more than two children.

Let's Talk Bahasa Indonesia

During the 1950s, soon after Indonesia became independent, Bahasa Indonesia was developed as a way of linking all Indonesians together. Here are some Bahasa Indonesia words to say:

selamat *(seh-LAHM-uht)*	*hello*
Selemat siang *(seh-LAHM-uht SYANG)*	*Good day*
Apa kabar? *(ah-puh-kuh-BAHR)*	*How are you?*
Nama saya … *(NAH-muh SIE-uh)*	*My name is …*
Saya dari … *(SIE-uh-DAH-ree)*	*I come from …*
Apa? *(AHP-uh)*	*What?*
Mengapa? *(maen-GAH-puh)*	*Why?*
tolong *(TOE-luhng)*	*please*
terima kasih *(tuh-REE-muh KAH-sih)*	*thank you*
ya *(YAH)*	*yes*
tidak *(TIH-dahk)*	*no*
selamat tinggal *(seh-LAHM-uht tihng-GAHL)*	*goodbye*

closed so that Muslims may go to their local mosque to pray, listen to preachers, and study Islam. Traditionally Indonesian mosques are built in a distinctive local style, with multi-story rooms and high, domed roofs. Their design is thought to be based on ancient Hindu *meru* (shrines). From the outside they look quite unlike mosques elsewhere in the world.

Followers of Islam in Indonesia also differ from other Muslims in their family lives and the way they dress. By law, Indonesian Muslim men may have only two wives, not four, as Muslim tradition normally allows. Many Indonesian Muslim women do not wear clothes that cover them completely from head to toe. They usually dress modestly, wearing headscarves, long-sleeved blouses, and skirts below the knee, but they do not veil their faces or wear long, voluminous robes. In many parts of Indonesia, Muslim beliefs have blended with earlier religious traditions, giving rise to many local religious legends. For example, Javanese legends tell how Islam was brought to the region by the Wali Songo—nine saints, or holy men, with magical powers.

Muslim boys on the island of Lombok sit on the floor to study the Islamic holy book, the Koran. Many Muslims can recite long passages from the Koran by heart.

during the holy month of Ramadan (RAH-muh-dahn) and hope to make a pilgrimage to Mecca (MEHK-uh) at least once during their lives. Friday is the Muslim holy day, and on Friday afternoons most government offices and many businesses are

Christianity

There are also Christian communities in Indonesia, although they make up only a small part of the population. About 5 percent of Indonesians are Protestants, and 3 percent are Roman Catholics. Christianity was brought to Indonesia during colonial times. Few Indonesians chose to become Christians, but those who did were offered a good, European-style education. This gave them an advantage over many other Indonesians, especially in the years soon after independence, when well-educated people were needed to help run the new nation. Even today Christians hold many senior posts in the army, civil service, and police.

Buddhists and Hindus

Buddhist and Hindu believers form even smaller minorities. Buddhists are mostly of Chinese descent and live in the business districts of cities and towns. The largest number of Hindus live on the island of Bali, where they follow a unique local version of the Hindu faith. Believers, known as *Agama* (uh-GAH-muh) Hindus,

Nyepi Festival

On the island of Bali, the Nyepi *(nee-EH-pee) Festival, held in late March or early April, marks the beginning of Hindu New Year. It starts on New Year's Eve, with prayers and religious ceremonies. Then processions of Balinese women offer food and flowers to the* ogoh-ogoh *(oe-GAWG-uh-goe) — a huge figure in the form of a monster, designed to scare away the evil spirits, displayed in each village square. Balinese men play music to accompany them. Everyone wears their best clothes, in traditional Balinese style. Then the ogoh-ogoh is paraded through the streets and in front of all the local temples. There are more prayers, and speeches are made by local leaders. By this time it is dark, and according to Balinese tradition, local spirits are lurking everywhere, so people make as much noise as they can with firecrackers, drums, and other musical instruments to drive them away. Then they burn the ogoh-ogoh figures on bonfires and enjoy a splendid feast that lasts all night long.*

Women on the island of Bali carrying offerings of food and flowers at the Nyepi Festival (Hindu New Year). They are wearing Balinese robes in brightly colored silk.

think that the world is full of forces that control everything, from volcanoes and earthquakes to individual human souls. Some are good, some are evil, and they are constantly at war. Some are invisible, but others take the form of kindly gods or wicked demons and witches. Agama Hindus believe that all these forces need to be kept in balance. They do this by making offerings of food, flowers, and music and by dancing to the good spirits and carrying out elaborate purification rituals using holy water to "kill" the evil spirits' power. They build beautiful temples as homes for the gods and invite them to visit by holding elaborate feasts and festivals. Dewi Sri (DAE-vee SREE), the goddess of rice, is a popular "guest," as is Ganesh (gah-NEHSH), the elephant-headed god "who makes things possible." Rangda (RAHNG-duh), the queen of demons, is hated and feared.

As well as following one of the official, state-recognized religions, most Indonesians also believe in animism, the ancient, original faith of the region. In some remote areas of Sumatra, Kalimantan, and Irian Jaya, animism remains the most important religion. Animists think that all living things, and many mountains, trees, and streams, have spirits that can help or harm them. They believe dead ancestors have spirits too, which can offer protection and advice to living members of their families and to the communities where they once lived. In Indonesia animists consult their ancestors or local nature-spirits before starting any important task. They ask *dunkuns* (doon-KOONS)—shamans, or spirit healers—to carry messages to the spirits.

A dunkun (shaman) from the Sukudei people. His skin is tattooed with magic patterns, and he wears a necklace of beads and bones.

Life on Sumatra

Sumatra is the sixth largest island in the world. It measures over 1,000 miles (1,600 kilometers) from end to end and covers an area of over 182,000 square miles (470,000 square kilometers). A range of mountains runs along the west coast. Many peaks are over 9,500 feet (3,000 meters) high, and fifteen of them are active volcanoes. The east of the island is low-lying, with wide, slow-flowing rivers and mangrove swamps along the coast. Large areas of Sumatra's natural rain forest vegetation have been cut down, but some of the original forests remain in the northern and west-central regions. Many rare and endangered wild animals live there, including unique local

249

Making cuts in the bark of a rain forest tree on the island of Sumatra. The thick, sticky sap that trickles from them is collected, then heated and dried to produce latex (natural rubber).

floor coverings and vehicle tires; the fruit of oil palms is crushed for oil that is used in food, cosmetics, and cleaning products. Hardwood trees from tropical forests are felled for timber and to make plywood. The most important crops are tea, coffee, cacao beans (used to make chocolate), pepper, and tobacco.

Over forty million people live in Sumatra, but compared with several other Indonesian islands, such as Bali and Java, it is sparsely inhabited, with a population density of around 219 people per square mile (85 per square kilometer). It is home to many different peoples, each with their

species such as the Sumatran tiger, the Sumatran rhino, orangutans, and honey bears. Rafflesia (ruh-FLEE-zhee-uh), the world's largest flower, also grows there.

Sumatra is rich in natural resources, including oil and natural gas. Rubber trees and oil palm trees are grown on vast plantations cleared from the rain forest. The sap of rubber trees is collected and processed to make

A water buffalo provides the power to pull this plow in northern Sumatra. Paddies, where rice is grown, are plowed every year after harvest to clear the land of weeds.

own culture. The largest groups include the Batak (BAW-tuhk), from the north, the Minangkabau (mihn-AHNG-kuh-bow), from the west, and the Mentawaians (mehn-tuh-WIE-uhnz), from islands just off the west coast. In the far north of Sumatra, the devoutly Muslim Atjehnese (AH-cheh-nees) people are calling for independence from Indonesian rule.

During the twentieth century the peoples of Sumatra, like all other Indonesians, saw rapid changes in their homelands caused by the introduction of modern technology and communications, economic development, and Western political and cultural ideas. Sometimes these changes completely destroyed traditional ways of life. For example, the Kubu (KOO-boo) people in the south of the island no longer live as nomadic hunters since the Indonesian government forcibly settled large numbers of migrants from crowded Bali and Java on their land. Today small groups of Kubu people live in a specially protected reserve. The rest of their forest hunting ground has been cut down to create plantations.

The Batak

The Batak have been more successful than the Kubu in maintaining their traditional lifestyle. About six million Batak people live in the mountains of northern Sumatra. They arrived there from Thailand and Burma (now Myanmar) over two thousand years ago. The rugged mountain countryside they chose for their new home meant that they lived cut off from the rest of Sumatra. They increased this isolation by refusing to build roads or bridges linking their villages to the outside world.

Each Batak community was hostile to outsiders, and rival villages fought long-lasting feuds. In the past, warriors ate the flesh of captured enemies or members of their own village who had committed serious offenses against adat (traditional law).

The Batak also fought against the Atjehnese, their neighbors to the north, who wanted to convert them to Islam. Most Batak never became Muslims, but many were converted to Christianity by Dutch missionaries in the nineteenth century. Today the majority of Batak are Protestant Christians, although they combine this faith with many animist beliefs. They make sacrifices to their ancestors' spirits and also to each person's *tondi* (TAWN-dee), or soul. The Batak believe that the soul sometimes leaves the body, causing illness and distress, and they believe that making offerings to it can persuade it to return. They are also famous for their moving choral performances of Christian hymns.

Traditional Batak houses are made of wood, carefully cut and shaped with hand tools and slotted together without nails. Their high, curving roofs with sharp pointed gables were originally made of palm fiber; today they are made of sheets of grooved iron. Houses are raised above the ground on stilts; the space underneath is used as a shelter for farm animals, such as cattle, hogs, and goats. Inside there is a large open space, divided by screens made of rattan (the woven stems of climbing tropical plants). Usually several Batak families share each house, but the village leader has a house of his own. Villages are surrounded by defensive ditches and strong walls made of bamboo poles.

Most Batak people live as farmers, raising animals, planting rice, and growing vegetables for their own use and to sell to consumers in Sumatra and abroad. Women do most of the work in the fields and also all the cooking, housework, and child care.

Batak men are skilled wood-carvers and metalworkers. They also make life-sized *sigalegale* puppets (wooden effigies), which are used to perform at funeral ceremonies and at weddings.

A Minangkabau house, with a traditional curving roof, in western Sumatra. Its wooden walls are richly decorated with paintings and carvings.

The Minangkabau

Farther south on the coast of western Sumatra the Minangkabau people live as farmers. They grow coffee, rice, and coconuts and raise cattle. Like the Batak, they build communal houses with high curving roofs, which they say look like water buffalo horns. They are mostly Muslims, but they also follow many traditional animist beliefs.

Many Minangkabau men leave their villages to work in industries elsewhere, especially coal mining. Minangkabau people are famous throughout Indonesia for their enterprising spirit and for the power their society gives to women; this is most unusual in Southeast Asia.

According to Minangkabau adat (laws), women head each family, and relationships with female family members (mother, grandmother, aunt) are more important than those with men. The oldest living woman is the head of each household, which might include several large families. She demands obedience and respect. Traditionally men have no rights over their wives, except to ask them to stay faithful. Fathers have no rights over their children either. If young people want male advice, they ask their mother's eldest brother, who also helps arrange marriages for them. When a young man marries, he moves into

Souls and Ghosts

The people of the Mentawai (mehn-TAH-wuh-ee) Islands, off the west coast of Sumatra, had little contact with the rest of the world until the twentieth century. As a result they, developed beliefs and traditions of their own. Many still survive today. For example, traditional healers on Mentawai say that good health and long life are brought by a happy soul. Sickness is caused when a soul leaves the body and can only be cured when it returns. They also believe that bad dreams occur because the soul slips away when a person goes to sleep. After death, the soul leaves a body forever and turns into a sanitu *(SA-nee-too), or angry ghost, who tries to steal souls from people who are still alive. Mentawai people guard the entrances to their homes and villages with magic sticks to keep these ghosts away.*

delicate gold and silver jewelry. In the past these items were made for their own use only; today they are sold to tourists to earn extra income.

Favorite Minangkabau entertainments include bullfights, horse races, acrobatic dances, and the *Randai* (ruhn-DIE), an exciting dance drama enacted at weddings. Performances are accompanied by gamelan (GA-mih-lan: an orchestra of gongs and drums) music and by bamboo flutes. *Pencak Silat* (pehn-CAHK sih-LAHT: martial arts) are also very popular among young men. These include mock battles and imitation fights with tigers.

Life on Java

Compared with neighboring Sumatra, Java is a fairly small island, with an area of 51,000 square miles (132,000 square kilometers), but it is the most densely inhabited region of Indonesia. Over 120 million people live there—over 50 percent of the country's population. It is a land of contrasts, with high mountains, including active volcanoes, along the center and in the west and fertile rice paddies on the coastal plains. Tea plantations are found on the lower mountain slopes. Java was the site of

his bride's family home, where he is expected to obey her older female relatives.

Minangkabau people are expert craftspeople, producing handwoven cloth in complicated patterns based on flowers, mountains, and trees. They also produce beautiful embroidery. Sometimes real gold and silver threads are included in the designs. Male craftworkers also produce

Baichaks (tricycle taxis) ready for hire in the big city of Surabaya, on the island of Java. They are powered by one person pedaling. It is exhausting work for little pay.

one of the word's worst volcanic eruptions, at Krakatau (krak-uh-TOW), in 1883 and has a famous active volcano, Bromo (BROE-moe). Java also has a few remaining areas of untouched natural rain forest, including the Kulon (KOO-lawng) Peninsula National Park, in the southwest, which is preserved as a World Heritage Site. Javanese single-horned rhinos live there. Extremely rare, there are less than one hundred of them left alive in the wild.

Indonesia's two largest cities have been built on Java's north coast—the capital, Jakarta, with a population of 17.5 million (including outlying districts), and the industrial center, Surabaya (suhr-uh-BIE-uh), with a population of 3 million. Jakarta is home of the Indonesian government, and most big businesses and international development organizations have their headquarters in the city. There are also two historic cities, Surakarta (suhr-uh-KAR-tuh) and Yogyakarta (yawg-yuh-KAR-tuh), which were both once capitals of ancient Javanese kingdoms. Today they are great tourist attractions. Visitors also flock to Java's magnificent Hindu and Buddhist temples.

Many different peoples live on Java. During the years when Indonesia's economy was growing fast, from around

The Explosion that Shook the World

One of the biggest volcanic eruptions happened on the Indonesian island of Krakatau, between Java and Sumatra, in August 1883. A series of massive explosions, lasting almost twenty-four hours, blasted several thousand tons of rock into the atmosphere. A tsunami, or tidal wave, 130 feet (40 meters) high, was sent rushing across the ocean. The sound could be heard over 2,500 miles (4,000 kilometers) away, and clouds of volcanic ash and dust released into the atmosphere disrupted the weather all around the world. At least 36,000 people were killed, and only one-third of Krakatau Island was left above sea level. Today there are 129 active volcanoes within Indonesia — more than anywhere else on earth — and scientists warn that another major eruption could happen at any time.

The island of Krakatau today. A new volcano, known as Anak (child of) Krakatau, is slowly rising from the shattered remains of the mountain that exploded in 1883.

Modern high-rise offices, hotels, and apartment buildings line Jalan Thamrin, the main highway in Jakarta, Indonesia's capital city.

1970 to 1997, hundreds of thousands of people moved to Java's big cities and towns from the countryside and remote islands, hoping to find work.

Traditionally Java was home to three different peoples: the Javanese, from the center and east of the island; the Madurese, from the northeast; and the Sundanese, from the west. As elsewhere in Indonesia, each had their own language and customs. These continue today, although most people speak Bahasa Indonesia, as well as their local language, and only observe traditional customs or wear traditional clothes on special occasions, such as weddings and community festivals. There

are many of these throughout the year, and they attract vast crowds of spectators. The most popular include bull races at Madura (MAHJ-uh-ruh) and kite flying at Pangandaran (PANG-duh-rahn).

For the rest of the time, especially in the cities, almost all the peoples of Java follow a modern lifestyle, working in offices, stores, and factories. They travel to their workplace on crowded buses, cars, and bicycles and relax at clubs, restaurants, cafés, and bars. In towns and cities people visit entertainment parks, botanic gardens, museums, theaters, and shopping malls. Jakarta has an amazing theme park, the Taman Mini Indonesia Indah, which contains rebuilt traditional houses from all the different regions of Indonesia, displays of regional crafts and clothes, and a vast boating lake containing small-scale models of all the main islands of the Indonesian archipelago.

Most Javanese families today live in modern houses made of concrete with sheet-metal roofs or in high-rise apartment buildings. Wealthy families live in spacious air-conditioned homes surrounded by beautiful gardens full of tropical flowers or in impressive colonial-style homes built by former Dutch rulers of Indonesia. Ordinary Indonesians' living conditions are often very crowded.

A few villages of traditional-style houses remain, where people follow their ancient way of life based on hunting and farming. For example, the Badui (BAW-dwee) people (a minority community living in the mountains of western Java) still build traditional thatched houses for ordinary families. The men grow nuts and fruit trees, and the women weave baskets and bags from dried rattan or tree bark. In the center of each Badui village, there is a special holy inner village, where animist priests and community elders live. They do not leave this inner village, preserving their religion, moral code, and general way of life, and only other Badui people can enter.

Bali

The island of Bali, to the east of Java, is one of the most beautiful in Indonesia. It is small, with an area of only 2,170 square miles (5,620 square kilometers), but it has a population density of around 1,152 people per square mile (445 per square kilometer). It has high mountains, lush green rice fields, and white sandy beaches fringed with coral reefs. The highest mountain, Gunung Agung (GOO-nuhng AE-goong), standing

Rice and palm trees growing in terraced fields on the island of Bali. Each terrace has been carefully cut out of the hillside by hand to stop heavy rains from washing the fertile soil away.

at 10,308 feet (3,142 meters), is an active volcano. To the south of this mountain, the gently sloping land is extremely fertile and has been shaped by Balinese farmers into narrow terraces to stop the soil from being washed away in heavy rains. In the north the land is more rugged, and coffee trees and coconut palms have been planted there. Farmers also grow vegetables and raise cattle. The island farms are very productive, but Bali is more famous as a vacation destination. Visitors travel here from many parts of the world, especially Australia and New Zealand, Europe, the United States, China, and Japan.

Tourism has brought prosperity to many Bali islanders, but it has also led to serious problems. New hotels and resort towns, built all around the coast, have driven villagers from their homes. They also occupy valuable farmland, making it difficult for Balinese people to grow enough food. Hotels and restaurants use vast amounts of water, even though Bali regularly suffers from drought. As a result, local people often run short of water for their families, their animals, and their crops. Tourist water sports, such as surfing, diving, and snorkeling, have damaged coral reefs and disturbed marine life. Tourists' cars and motorbikes damage narrow local roads and cause air pollution. Many local people also feel that the constant stream of visitors to their villages, homes, and ancient temples is ruining their quality of life.

In spite of these problems most Balinese people are determined to maintain their traditional lifestyle and to continue their local customs and adat. They are proud of their unique culture, which is based on their Hindu religious beliefs. The local Balinese language is also strongly influenced by religion—it can be spoken in five different ways, depending on the caste (religious rank) of the speakers' and listeners' families.

Bali's society is organized around villages. Each Balinese man, woman, and child feels strong loyalty to their village as well as to their family and clan. They are brought up to believe that anything they do wrong will harm their whole village community and bring great shame on themselves. Special village organizations arrange marriages, funerals, village festivals, and manage the network of irrigation ditches that carry water to the terraced rice fields. A village contains several homes, each standing in its own compound (courtyard), which is surrounded by a high wooden wall. Inside each compound there is a small family temple, a garden, and several *bale*, which are typical Balinese buildings consisting of a rectangle of pounded earth or a low platform, covered by a high, steep roof supported on wooden pillars. Each bale has a separate function—for example, sleeping, cooking, or washing. All villages also have a *bale banjar* (bah-lih-bahn-JAHR), a large, open-sided building used for community events such as concerts and feasts.

Most Balinese villages have at least three temples: one, next to the graveyard, honors ancestor spirits; one honors the men and women who founded the village hundreds of years ago; and one is for the spirits that guard the village today. The Balinese believe that Hindu gods and other spirits

Windsurfers enjoy ideal conditions on a beach in Bali. Many people come to Indonesia to surf huge ocean breakers and to dive among its beautiful coral reefs.

visit the temples on festival days, and the Balinese welcome them with music, dancing, and dramatic plays. Bali's dancers are famous throughout Indonesia; often their dances retell ancient Hindu legends or other popular stories. Dancers wear beautiful costumes based on traditional Balinese sarongs (suh-RAWNGZ) — lengths of cloth wrapped tightly around the body — richly decorated with woven patterns in silver and gold. Movements — especially of the head and hands — are delicate, slow, and stylized, producing a very graceful effect. Dramatic facial expressions are another important part of the performance. Musicians in Bali have their own special way of playing gamelan music. It is very popular all over the island.

Balinese crafts include wood and stone carvings, originally used to decorate temples and other important buildings. Many feature religious designs or scenes from everyday life.

Dancers performing the Legon *on Bali. This traditional dance, using swift movements, tells the dramatic story of a king and princess who lived long ago.*

Kalimantan

The Indonesian region of Kalimantan consists of the southern two-thirds of the vast island of Borneo, an area of nearly 200,000 square miles (500,000 square kilometers). The landscape is inhospitable, with steep mountain ranges in the center of the island and also in the far southeast. The rest of the land is mostly low lying and crossed by wide rivers. Indonesia's longest river, the Kapuas (KAWP-uh-was), flows for about 750 miles (1,200 kilometers), reaching the sea at Pontianak (pahn-tee-AH-nahk), in the northeast.

Until recently, most of Kalimantan was covered in dense rain forest, with tangled mangrove swamps where rivers and forests met the sea. There were few roads or bridges, so the rivers were used as highways to and from the coast. Cross-country journeys were almost impossible. Even today there are few good roads or river crossings in inland Kalimantan, although Australian aid agencies have supplied thousands of lightweight, easy-to-build metal bridges to help local people cross smaller streams and mountain ravines. There are several new national and provincial airports and many good harbors, so it is easier to travel inland by plane or around the coast by boat.

Kalimantan means "river of gems," and the east of the island has rich deposits of diamonds and gold. There are also vast resources of oil, natural gas, and coal. In the late twentieth century the Indonesian government encouraged mining and processing businesses to work in the region along with

Forest Fires

In 1997 and 1998 huge forest fires raged in the Indonesian region of Kalimantan. Their smoke blanketed neighboring countries from Thailand to the Philippines in a choking cloud of smog.

The blaze spread after small fires, started by local farmers using traditional slash-and-burn techniques, got out of control. They were made worse by fires from illegal logging operations and by unusually dry weather conditions. These forest fires were a disaster for people, wildlife, and plants. Millions of men, women, and children fell ill with chest infections and skin diseases. Large areas of rain forest were destroyed, along with countless wild animals, insects, and birds. The smog disrupted air travel and caused massive traffic jams on roads. It also caused acid rain to fall in many parts of Southeast Asia, leading to further damage to fragile forests, rivers, streams, and coastal coral reefs.

Surrounded by clouds of dense, choking smoke, firefighters and volunteers try to stop a forest blaze from spreading in Kalimantan, on the island of Borneo.

timber companies. Uncontrolled drilling, mining, and logging has led to serious environmental damage and has threatened many species of wildlife, including orangutans, clouded leopards, and giant hornbills (huge birds with massive beaks traditionally believed to have magic powers). Rare rain forest trees are also under threat. Kalimantan is home to over five thousand different hardwood species as well as hundreds of beautiful orchids and giant butterflies. Crocodiles, otters, snakes, and many kinds of fish live in the rivers.

Around nine million people live on Kalimantan. The three largest ethnic groups are the Malays, Dayak (the original inhabitants), and Chinese. Small numbers of Malay people moved to Kalimantan at various times throughout the past four hundred years. They settled in coastal cities and along the banks of major rivers, working on boats and as general laborers. Before independence some were also employed by British and Dutch oil and rubber companies. Nearly all were Muslims, and they lived fairly peacefully alongside ethnic Chinese who ran many stores and other businesses in coastal cities, as they still do today. Neither group had much contact with the Dayak, who lived mostly inland in inaccessible mountain regions.

During the late twentieth century the Indonesian government encouraged large

Dayak men on Borneo collecting tough, flexible stems from the rain forest. The stems, called rattan, can grow up to 300 feet (90 meters) long and are woven into baskets and used to make furniture.

numbers of Malay *transmigrasi* settlers to move to Kalimantan. There they work in the mining and logging industries and on rubber and oil palm plantations. They often clash with local Dayak people, who accuse them of taking their land. Other new inhabitants include foreign technical experts working for oil and mining companies. They often live in company compounds, protected from the world outside by patrolling guards and strong fences.

The name *Dayak* is used to describe many different groups of local people who have lived in Borneo for over four thousand years. Most are farmers who use slash-and-burn techniques to clear small patches of rain forest for planting crops like taro (TAH-roe) — an edible root — and vegetables. They carry away the felled trees to build their houses and set fire to the bushy undergrowth to reveal the uncultivated earth of the forest floor. The ash from the fire also helps to enrich the soil. After a few seasons they abandon the cleared plot, but it takes many years for the rain forest to grow back again. The Dayak also gather many wild foods, including fruits, nuts, and honey, from the rain forest and use guns or traditional blowpipes with poison-tipped darts to kill wild animals and birds. They use the meat for food, the skins to make useful containers, and wear the feathers as body decoration.

A few Dayak groups, such as the Punan (poo-NAHN), are nomads who spend all their time hunting in the forest. Most other Dayak live in settled villages in forest clearings or on riverbanks. Traditionally the

A Dayak hunter uses a stone to sharpen the iron blade of his spear. Dayak people still use traditional weapons to hunt wild animals, especially hogs, in the Borneo rain forest.

Tiwah Ceremony

On the island of Kalimantan, Dayak people hold the Tiwah *(tih-WAH) to help and honor their ancestors. Small Tiwah ceremonies usually take place twice a year, with a special, splendid ceremony about once every five years. At Tiwah families move the bones of relatives who have recently died from their first, temporary grave to a permanent resting place. They believe this also helps the dead peoples' spirits to escape from their bodies and move on to the next world. The bones are first washed, then purified in special ceremonies. This "cleans" them from any sins the dead person might have committed. Animals and birds are sacrificed to help nourish the spirits. Finally the purified bones are carried to the* sandung *(suhn-DOONG), a house-shaped container on tall poles, where they remain.*

Dayak live in large windowless longhouses built from wood and thatched with dried plants. Longhouses are raised above the ground on stilts to protect the inhabitants from sudden attack. The only way in is by ladder. Several families live in each longhouse; some are large enough for a whole village community to sleep in.

For centuries the Dayak have had a fearsome reputation as headhunters. Traditionally Dayak warriors cut off and kept the heads of enemies they had killed in battle. According to animist beliefs, this meant that the dead enemy's spirit would help and strengthen them rather than return to haunt them and do them harm. The custom of head-hunting still continues — although rarely — today, even though many Dayak have become Christians. As elsewhere in Indonesia, they combine their new faith with many ancient traditions.

Dayak crafts include woodworking, carving masks (worn in animist ceremonies), and making weapons such as blowpipes and *mandau* (muhn-DOW) — machetes used for clearing paths through forest undergrowth. Dayak women also weave sarongs from the bark of rain forest trees. In the past Dayak women wore big earrings of brass or gold. Many were so heavy that they made huge holes in their earlobes, stretching the skin so much the lobes touched the women's shoulders. Dayak women also decorated their arms and legs with tattoos portraying magic birds and spirits. Dayak men who had captured enemy heads also wore tattoos as a sign of honor. Today these customs are disappearing fast, since they are strongly discouraged by the Indonesian government and by Christian missionaries.

Proud of her ancient heritage, this elderly Dayak woman displays her tattooed arms. Over the years, her earlobes have been stretched by the weight of metal earrings.

This house belonging to a Bugi family on the island of Sulawesi is built in traditional style, with a thatched roof. It is raised above the ground on wooden poles.

Sulawesi

Lying to the east of Kalimantan, Sulawesi is much more mountainous and smaller at around 72,775 square miles (188,487 square kilometers). The island is divided into four narrow peninsulas, each with its own separate character. No settlement is much farther than 60 miles (100 kilometers) from the sea and, traditionally, boats were the best way to travel. However, as the tourist industry expanded in the 1990s, many new roads were built across the mountains and along the coast.

Sulawesi is home to an astonishing variety of wildlife, including tiny dwarf water buffalo, deer hogs (hogs with long legs and huge curving tusks), 62 species of bats, and 328 different kinds of birds. Dolphins, dugongs (doo-GAWNGZ) or sea cows, and many brilliantly colored fish live

in the coral reefs offshore. As elsewhere in Indonesia, many land animals are endangered by destruction of their habitats; the sea creatures are under threat from uncontrolled fishing and tourism.

Many different peoples live on Sulawesi, including the Bugis (BUHG-ihs) and the Makassarese (muh-kuhs-sah-REH-see), in the south; the Toraja (toe-RAH-jah), in the center; and the Minahasans (mee-nuh-HAHS-uhnz), in the north. There are also communities of Bajau (BAH-jaw), also known as sea

Cash for Coconuts

The northern half of the island of Sulawesi is densely covered by coconut palm trees. These form the basis of the local economy, making Sulawesi one of the wealthiest of Indonesia's remote regions. Coconuts are grown for food — their juice is drunk fresh locally; and their flesh is processed into an important ingredient in many sweet and savory dishes worldwide. Coconuts and the trees they grow on also yield many other useful products, including oil (used in soaps, cosmetics, detergents, and explosives), tough fibers (used for mats and ropes), timber (used for building), leaves (which are dried and woven into baskets and hats or used to thatch roofs), and husks, which are shelled and used as a garden fertilizer. In Indonesia dried coconut shells are also burned as fuel, and fresh leaves are used as disposable plates.

gypsies. The total population is around 6.5 million, the Bugis forming the largest group. Traditionally they, and the Makassarese, were sailors who made long voyages to trade—sometimes reaching Australia about 700 miles (1,100 kilometers) away. Today many Bugi and Makassarese people still work as sailors, traders, and boatbuilders and are based in the busy port of Ujung Pandang (OO-jang PAH-duhng), formerly known as Makassar, and other harbors along the south coast. Others are farmers, growing corn and palm trees or raising silkworms. Many work as fishers or make salt by evaporating seawater in the hot sun. Some find employment as guides, drivers, cooks, and hotel workers in the tourist industry.

Most Bugis and Makassarese are Muslims, but they still follow some traditional animist beliefs. They are famous for their independent opinions, and they have rebelled against Indonesian government policies several times.

The Bajau people also make their living from the sea, by diving to collect sea cucumbers (a kind of sea slug prized by Chinese cooks), corals, and pearls. Many Bajau spend their whole lives on boats at sea, sailing from place to place to find work. Others live in clusters of offshore houses, perched on tall stilts, standing in the water close to reefs or shallow lagoons. Traditionally a Bajau baby is given its first swimming lesson at three days old!

The Toraja people of central Sulawesi follow a very different way of life. They are farmers, raising water buffalo, hogs, and chickens, growing rice in irrigated fields and also coffee, cotton, and sugarcane. Their villages of splendid wooden houses are raised on stilts. The houses have enormous overhanging roofs that look like upturned boats. Traditionally roofs were made of bamboo, but today sheets of iron are more common. The walls of each house are painted with geometric patterns in brilliant colors. Each design has its own special meaning and is believed to protect

The huge, boat-shaped roofs of four traditional houses, built by the Toraja people in central Sulawesi, create a dramatic skyline.

the people inside. The front of each house is decorated with a water buffalo head carved in wood. Water buffalo are symbols of wealth and power for the Toraja. Underneath each house is a wooden platform used as a meeting place. For storing rice many houses have several small granaries close by, built in a similar style.

The Toraja people met few outsiders before the twentieth century. Today they still observe many traditional rituals and festivals, even though many of them are Christians. Funerals are especially important: the Toraja believe that without them a dead person's spirit can never find rest. Soon after a death families hold a funeral feast. The dead person's body, preserved by herbs or modern chemicals, is present and seated in the place of honor as if they were still alive. There are solemn songs and dances before the preserved body is buried in the family tomb, which is often in a cave. Months or years later, as soon as the family can afford it, a second funeral is held. Valuable animals,

Carved wooden statues of Toraja family ancestors in Sulawesi stand outside the wooden doorways attached to caves where their bones are buried.

especially water buffalo, are sacrificed, so that their spirits can help the dead person on their long journey to heaven. A lifelike wooden statue of them is also placed outside. Many families spend so much on these offerings that the Indonesian government has tried to limit them by law.

Spice Islands of Maluku

The province of Maluku consists of hundreds of islands scattered across a vast expanse of sea to the east of Sulawesi. The total area is 328,000 square miles (850,000 square kilometers), but only one-tenth of it is land. Most islands are mountainous and covered with rain forest. There are many active volcanoes, and earthquakes, lava flows, and other volcanic eruptions are common. The wildlife is a mixture of Asian and Australian species, including monkeys, parrots, and kangaroos. Top-quality hardwood trees, rare today but used in the past to make fine furniture, grow wild in the forests, together with wonderful orchids.

About two million people live in Maluku. Early settlers were Malays,

Fishing from canoes off the southernmost islands in the Maluku region. Ambon, the largest town in the Spice Islands, was once a center of the international spice trade.

Papuans, Hawaiians, and people from Polynesian islands. Later arrivals included traders from Java and China and the seafaring Bugi people from Sulawesi. After around 1500 there were also European settlers, mostly from Portugal and the Netherlands. Today many Maluku people are of mixed ancestry. Around half the population is Christian; the rest is Muslim. Christians live mostly on the southern islands; Muslims live in the north. In 1999 there were violent clashes between Christians and Muslims on the island of Ambon (AHM-bawn). A few communities, such as the Papuan Nuaulu (NWAH-loo) and Alifur (ah-lih-FOOR) people on the island of Seram (sae-RAHM), continue their ancient traditions. These include slash-and-burn agriculture, hunting with blowpipes and spiked traps, and wrestling.

Most people in Maluku work as farmers, laborers, and traders. For many centuries Maluku was known as the Spice Islands. Cloves, nutmeg, pepper, cinnamon, and many other spices were grown there and sold around the world. Today clove and nutmeg trees are still cultivated, but farmers in Maluku also grow cacao beans, coffee, and bananas for export, as well as rice and vegetables to feed their families. They collect sago (SAE-goe), the pith of a spiky palm tree that grows wild on the islands. This is boiled, then pounded into flat, starchy cakes that can be steamed or fried.

In the southern islands many people earn a living from fishing and from felling timber. There are also oil wells and a growing tourist industry based on water sports, which employs a large number of people.

Nusa Tenggara (Southeast Islands)

The largest and most important islands of Nusa Tenggara (noo-suh-tehn-GAH-ruh) are Lombok, Sumbawa (soom-BAH-wuh), Flores, Sumba (SOOM-bah), and Timor. Only the western half of Timor belongs to Indonesia; the eastern half became an independent nation (see EAST TIMOR) in 2002. The islands are mostly mountainous, and the land is rugged and dry. There are many volcanoes, and in 1815 Gunung Tambora (TAM-boe-ruh) on Sumbawa exploded in the largest volcanic eruption in recorded history. Wildlife includes the world's largest lizard, the Komodo (kuh-MOED-oe) dragon. It grows to over 10 feet (3 meters) long and can weigh over 220 pounds (100 kilograms). Only about 2,500 survive in the wild, making it a protected species.

Compared with many regions of Indonesia, Nusa Tenggara is sparsely populated. Around eight million people live there—almost half on Lombok, which is the most developed and crowded island in Nusa Tenggara. The majority of people in the region are ethnic Malays, but there are Melanesian communities on the eastern islands. Both Malays and Melanesians are divided into many different groups, each with their own separate language, culture, and traditions. There are at least sixty different languages, plus many local dialects.

In coastal towns there are communities of Muslim sailors and traders from Sulawesi; small groups of Arabs, also descended from

On the island of Sumba, in Nusa Tenggara, men wear traditional head coverings and colorful woven cloaks for the Pasola festival.

traders; settlers from Bali (who live mostly in Lombok, the nearest island to their home); and Chinese people who run businesses on most Nusa Tenggara islands. In the late twentieth century the Indonesian government also encouraged groups of transmigrasi laborers from Java and Bali to settle in Nusa Tenggara.

The peoples of western Nusa Tenggara are Muslims. From the island of Flores eastward they are mostly Christians. There are a small number of Hindus, mostly Balinese, on Lombok. Many traditional beliefs also survive, including ancestor worship, animal sacrifice, and trials of strength among warriors. Communities celebrate many traditional festivals, such as Pasola (PAH-soe-luh) on Sumba, where riders on horseback take part in mock battles. Originally these were fought with real weapons; people believed that the blood from dead and wounded contestants pleased the local spirits and guaranteed a good harvest. Today the weapons are blunt, but warriors still often get hurt.

Throughout the region people cling to their traditional values, such as respect for elders and loyalty to family or clan. They respect the *kepala desa* (keh-PAH-luh DAE-suh), or village head, who organizes day-to-day life, and also the *kepala suku* (SOO-koo), or clan chief, who organizes traditional rituals. Among the Betu (BAE-too) people on Timor, many communities

The Nyale Fishing Festival

The Nyale Fishing Festival marks the beginning of the fishing season on the Nusa Tenggara island of Lombok. Traditionally a good catch of fish is believed to predict a plentiful rice harvest later in the year.

In February or March crowds of young people gather on the beach at Kuta (KOO-tuh). They build bonfires and spend all night sitting around them, making up humorous rhymes. The next day, at dawn, fishing boats set out in search of nyale *(nee-AH-lee), a fish shaped like a fat worm. As soon as the first nyale is caught, the young people swim out or climb into boats and chase each other around the bay. They catch nyale fish and either eat them raw or cook them over the beach fires.*

are headed by women, who also own most of the property.

Many families in Nusa Tenggara still live in traditional houses. Each local community has its own style, but on most islands homes are very large and are designed to house several families. They are often raised above the ground on stilts to keep clear of flooding and have several stories, each with a different purpose. The main living area is on the second floor, with spaces screened off for cooking and sleeping. The loft is used for storage; the first floor is for keeping animals. Houses are made of wood and roofed with thatch. Roofs are often very high and steeply sloped; timber posts and doorways can be elaborately carved.

There are exceptions to this general pattern. In Timor the Dawan (dah-WAHN) people build small, cone-shaped houses, completely covered in thatch, with no windows and a doorway just high enough to crawl through. On Lombok many families live in modern houses made of concrete blocks and roofed with grooved sheets of iron, but villagers still build communal meeting houses and buildings used for animist ceremonies in traditional timber and thatch style.

Nusa Tenggara is the poorest region of Indonesia. Its dry climate and thin soils mean that wet rice (the chief food crop of Indonesia) will not grow there except in a few small areas. Farmers plant dry rice (grown without irrigation), corn, and taro (an edible root) and gather sago from wild palm trees. Most families survive by subsistence farming, managing to grow just enough food to keep themselves alive. They also find work as laborers on large plantations, often owned by foreign investors, where coffee, cotton, and coconuts are grown. Some Nusa Tenggara farmers grow crops to sell for export,

Fishers from the island of Lombok haul their catch on board a prahu (traditional outrigger canoe). The wooden rigs (frames) on each side give it stability in rough seas.

including coffee, onions, pineapples, tobacco, and cashew nuts. They also raise cattle, water buffalo, horses, chickens, and hogs.

Families living on the coast make a living from fishing and, increasingly, from the tourist industry. The island of Lombok is a popular vacation destination. Visitors come to relax on its beautiful beaches or to climb Gunung Rinjani (rihn-JAH-nee), an active volcano with a dramatic crater lake. Traditional crafts sold to tourists, especially pottery made on Lombok, are an important source of income, and the mining industry is also developing fast. There is a new gold mine on the island of Sumbawa, and oil companies are prospecting in the Timor Sea.

Irian Jaya

Irian Jaya is the western half of the island of New Guinea. It covers the vast area of 162,928 square miles (421,984 square kilometers), and the landscape is harsh and rugged. A range of high mountains runs along the center of the island. Although they are close to the equator, the highest peaks remain covered with snow year-round, and there are grassy pastures on their upper slopes. The lower mountains are covered with dense rain forest, which also covers the narrow strip of flatland along the northern coast. On the edge of the ocean the main vegetation is coconut palms. Rain forest also grows on the low-lying land in the south of the island, but there are large areas of mangrove swamp here and thickets of sago palms. Wildlife includes snakes, lizards, possums, tree wallabies, and over eight hundred species of spiders. The rare and beautiful bird of paradise (a bird with beautifully colored plumes) also lives in the rain forests.

Irian Jaya has only been ruled by Indonesia since 1963. (It remained a Dutch colony after the rest of the country gained independence in 1949.) For this reason, and because of its remoteness, ruggedness, and vast size, it is largely undeveloped, and many of its people still continue with their traditional way of life. There are about two million inhabitants. Most are Papuans, living inland in small and isolated communities, each with their own customs and languages. There may be over seven hundred languages spoken in Irian Jaya; many have not yet been studied by outsiders.

Around the coasts there are small groups of Malays, Melanesians, and people of mixed ancestry. There is a large Indonesian naval base on the north coast, and the Indonesian government has also allowed many foreign companies to set up mining and logging enterprises. As well as causing environmental problems, this has provoked anger among the Irian Jayans.

Christian missionaries arrived in Irian Jaya during the twentieth century, and today most Papuans are Christians. However, they continue to hold many animist beliefs and to follow traditional customs, such as ritual battles to settle quarrels between neighboring people or cutting off a fingertip when a close relative dies. Papuan men could traditionally marry as many wives as they liked, so long as they could pay the price for them—a gift of several hogs to the bride's father. Although the custom of having many wives, called polygamy, is against Indonesian law, it is still widespread today. Malay and Melanesian people, including the transmigrasi settlers, are mostly Muslims, and there are mosques in many coastal towns.

Many Papuans, such as the Dani (DAH-nee) people, who live away from the coast, survive by raising hogs and planting crops of sweet potatoes. Men use simple stone tools to clear fields and dig irrigation ditches. Women plant and care for the crops and harvest them. Papuans also gather wild fruits and nuts from the rain forest and hunt wild animals there, using blowpipes and bows and arrows. They live in villages, often consisting of several family compounds—groups of low, round, or square homes built of tree branches and mud. However, some Papuan peoples prefer to build houses on stilts or even high in trees. This protects them from surprise attacks by wild animals and enemy warriors.

In Irian Jaya's coastal towns most men and women wear Western-style clothing or simple sarongs, as do other people throughout Indonesia, but many Papuans prefer to dress in traditional style. For men, this means few garments but many decorative items, such as feather

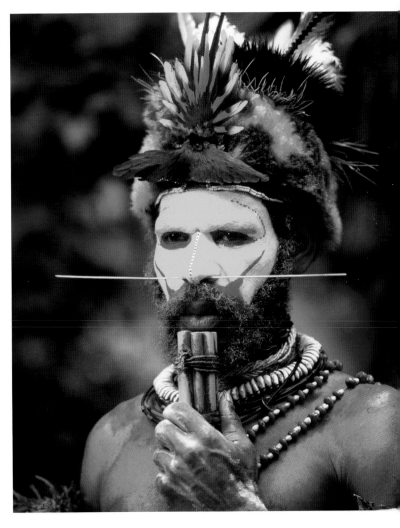

A hunter from the Huli people of Irian Jaya holds a set of musical pipes to his lips. He has painted his face and has pierced his nose with a sharp quill.

The Dani people of Irian Jaya use feathers from brightly colored rain forest birds to create splendid headdresses and necklaces.

headdresses and cowrie shell necklaces. Many men also spread hog fat over their skin and in their hair; this helps them keep warm, and they also believe it brings good health. They also paint patterns on their faces and bodies using soot. Papuan women wear skirts made of grass if they are unmarried and seeds and twisted plant fiber if they have a husband. Many traditional Papuan crafts are designed to be worn or carried, such as bracelets woven from dyed rattan (rain forest vines), bags and nets made from tree bark, carved wooden shields, and jewelry made from shells and feathers.

Building a New Nation

When Indonesia became independent in 1949, its first president, Achmed Sukarno, declared that his new nation should be guided by Pancasila (Five Principles). He hoped these ideas would prove acceptable to all Indonesians whatever their ethnic origin, local loyalties, or religious faith and that his ideas would help unite all Indonesians.

Governments since Sukarno have continued to proclaim Pancasila as the basis of the Indonesian state, even though critics of the government claim that some of its ideas, especially social justice, have not yet been realized. Indonesian governments have constantly been accused of inefficiency and corruption, nepotism (unjustly favoring family members), and cronyism (giving unfair help to political colleagues and friends). The legal system and financial institutions, such as banks, have also been accused of corrupt practices. This means that many Indonesian people—and foreign companies seeking to develop businesses in Indonesia—cannot draw up effective contracts (legal agreements), manage their finances, collect debts, or get a fair trial.

The army and police have also been accused of many human rights abuses, especially during the occupation of East Timor. Army and police officers have regularly interfered in politics or worked to help wealthy, powerful families. Elections have been neither free nor fair, allowing authoritarian leaders like Sukarno and Suharto to stay in power.

The Indonesian government has also faced natural hazards, such as earthquakes and floods. They have failed to stop environmental damage caused by logging and mining companies and by insensitive tourist developments on many islands. They have clashed with religious fundamentalists and separatist movements, and their corrupt, authoritarian policies have also led to quarrels with other nations and with international organizations offering development aid or supporting human rights.

There are hopes that the new government, which was elected in 2001 and is headed by Megawati Sukarnoputri, will end these political, legal, and financial abuses and introduce reforms, but this remains to be seen.

For the moment Indonesian society remains varied and often unequal. People living in different regions have different lifestyles and different standards of living, opportunities for employment, and access to education and health care. The difference is greatest between wealthy islands, such as Java and Bali, and more remote regions, such as Nusa Tenggara and Irian Jaya. Keeping this vast nation together is a serious challenge for the Indonesian government. Indonesia also faces major economic problems.

From soon after independence in 1949 until 1997, the Indonesian economy was booming. Encouraged by President

Suharto, who liked to call himself "the father of development," many new businesses were set up and millions of new jobs were created. Suharto's economic policies were supported by powerful international development agencies, such as the World Bank (a specialist United Nations agency).

During that time Indonesia changed from being mainly a producer of raw materials to a promising center of manufacturing and industry. Indonesia is rich in natural resources, such as oil, natural gas, timber, rubber, coffee, tea, and many minerals, including tin, nickel, bauxite, copper, coal, silver, and gold. From the 1970s these were processed within the country as well as being exported. Indonesia also made industrial products, including cement, chemical fertilizers, and plywood, and had many factories making textiles, clothing, and footwear. Tourism became increasingly important. In spite of this rapid

At a mine in Irian Jaya men and women stand waist-deep in muddy water as they pan (search) for nuggets of gold, a major export in Indonesia.

development, half the Indonesian population still worked on the land, on plantations, or as subsistence farmers, growing food for themselves and their families.

In 1997 Indonesia was badly damaged by the economic crisis that affected almost all of East Asia. This, together with the unstable political situation, led to a sudden slump in the value of the Indonesian currency, the Indonesian rupiah (roo-PEE-uh). As a result, many businesses went bankrupt and collapsed. Millions of workers lost their jobs, and prices rose rapidly, even for essential foods. It looked as if many poor families would go hungry and lose their homes. To limit the damage, the International Monetary Fund (a United Nations agency) took over the running of the Indonesian economy. Its tough policies, designed also to attack corruption, led to further price increases, and in 1998 there were serious riots. Many food stores, especially those run by Chinese families, were looted and destroyed.

A scavenger hunts for useful items in a polluted river clogged by garbage and driftwood in Indonesia's capital city, Jakarta.

Since 1997 economies throughout East Asia have slowly recovered. The economic situation in Indonesia has improved as well, boosted by high world prices for oil and gold. Indonesia's wealth also comes from tourism, transportation and other service industries, mining, logging and other industries, and agriculture. Over 40 percent of the population still works on the land; about 40 percent works in service industries; and 16 percent works in

industry. There are still problems, however. Foreign businesses remain unwilling to invest in Indonesian developments; the Indonesian government has massive debts; and inflation is quite high at around 9 percent per year.

Economic problems have left a legacy of social, political, and environmental difficulties. Millions of poor families have left their homes in the country to look for work in cities, where they live in miserable, crowded, and unhealthy conditions. Uncontrolled factory and house building has led to air and water pollution and to traffic congestion in towns. Illegal logging and forest burning has created vast smog clouds.

Since the 1997 economic crisis, the gap between rich and poor has increased. The richest 10 percent of Indonesian families possess almost 30 percent of the nation's wealth, while one in four people lives below the poverty line, without adequate food, housing, education, or health care. Big cities, like the national capital Jakarta, have leafy suburbs with comfortable villas, shopping malls, and elegant high-rise apartment buildings. These are right

beside squalid slums where people live in flimsy homes with no clean water, bathrooms, or drains.

Shared Values

In spite of all these differences and difficulties, the peoples of Indonesia still share many of the same values and hopes, such as a respect for family life. Most Indonesian families are large and include aunts, uncles, cousins, and other more distant kin as well as parents, grandparents, and children. In the countryside a family might include all the inhabitants of a communal longhouse or everyone in a small village.

Many Indonesians work together in family businesses or on family farms. Indonesian people also like to spend their

A shantytown on the outskirts of Indonesia's capital, Jakarta. Thousands of families live here in flimsy riverside homes with no clean water or sewerage.

free time with their families, working together, sharing a meal, strolling in a large, talkative group through a market or along a beach.

Families provide practical and emotional support and a comforting sense of identity and belonging. Family elders demand respect and obedience. In return they help younger members get an education, find a job, and choose a marriage partner. For all these reasons children are brought up to think that their own individual tastes, wishes, and feelings are less important than loyalty to their family group.

In general most Indonesian people do not value solitude, privacy, or silence—unless they want to study or concentrate on their work. Instead they are often keen to meet and talk with strangers, are used to sharing, and are friendly and hospitable. Traditionally it is important for senior men and women not to "lose face"—that is, not to look awkward or foolish in front of others—especially in business meetings,

when dealing with officials, in colleges, or at school. For this reason tact and good manners are considered important.

Education and Health Care

Most people value education because it provides opportunities for well-paying jobs and interesting careers. Schools are run by the state and also by mosques and churches. There are three grades: primary (elementary), for children 6 to 12 years old; junior high (12 to 15 year olds); and senior high (15 to 18 year olds). According to the law, education is open to all, but it is not free. Parents have to pay for school fees, books, and uniforms. These are not expensive, but the cost is still too high for many ordinary families to afford. As a result, few children stay on beyond elementary school. They leave around the

A class of boys outside their school in a village on the island of Bali. Three out of every four Indonesians can read and write.

age of twelve to help their parents at work or to care for the family home and their younger brothers and sisters. For wealthy families who can afford to keep their children at school, Indonesia has many colleges and universities. The most prestigious are on the island of Java.

Indonesia is a young country. Over one-third of the population is under fourteen years of age. On average, an Indonesian boy can expect to live until he is about sixty-five and a girl until she is seventy. Most Indonesian mothers will have two or maybe three children, but these average figures conceal big differences between the health of rich people and the poor.

Everyone living in Indonesia runs the risk of contracting several serious diseases that can sometimes be fatal, but the risk is higher for poor people and for families living in rural areas. The most dangerous diseases include malaria and dengue fever, carried by mosquitoes; rabies, transmitted by animal bites; and hepatitis, cholera, and typhus, caused by drinking polluted water. Other unpleasant ailments, such as intestinal parasites, are also carried by dirty water and uncooked food. Doctors have estimated that eight out of every ten people in rural Indonesia suffer from flukes (worms). They cause serious stomach upsets, weakness, and exhaustion.

There are also many insects and other wild creatures with dangerous bites and stings, including ticks and leeches (that both suck blood), spiders, scorpions, and poisonous snakes. Around the coasts there are poisonous fish, sea snakes, crocodiles, and sharks.

The Indonesian diet, which is based on fresh fruits, vegetables, and starchy foods such as rice, is basically very healthy, but a large number of poor Indonesian families do not get enough to eat, and this increases their risk of illness. Unhealthy living

conditions, caused by smog, polluted water, and lack of sanitation, as well as lack of refrigeration and clean food preparation facilities in many slums and country districts, also increase the risk of disease spreading. There is a growing problem of drug abuse—Indonesia is used as a crossroads point for buying and selling drugs grown elsewhere in Southeast Asia. Also, infection with HIV/AIDS is on the rise.

There are good private hospitals in Indonesian cities, but only rich people can afford to use them. There are also hospitals funded by the state or run by charities in smaller towns, and there are health-care clinics in remote districts, but many Indonesian families live out of reach of adequate health care. They rely on traditional healers using herbs and animist rituals for help. In towns many people consult practitioners in Chinese traditional medicine.

Food and Drink

Like the Indonesian land and the Indonesian people, Indonesian food is varied. In the wealthy districts of big cities and towns there are well-stocked stores and open-air markets, smart restaurants serving Indonesian, Chinese, and Indian food, and also Western-style coffee bars and branches of international doughnut and burger chains, but in poorer city districts and many parts of the countryside food is simpler, more traditional, and, sometimes, in short supply.

For almost all Indonesians, rich or poor, rice, or *nasi* (NAHS-ee), is the staple food, eaten at most meals. Much Indonesian rice is a special glutinous variety that goes soft and sticky when cooked. Traditionally diners use the fingers of their right hand to shape a small portion of sticky rice into a

A fine variety of vegetables for sale at a market in Kalimantan, on the island of Borneo. If possible, most Indonesians like to shop for fresh food every day.

Sago and taro are two traditional foods still widely eaten in country districts of Indonesia. They are bland-tasting, starchy, and filling; usually they are served as a background for small amounts of spicy, strongly flavored food. Sago is the pith of a spiky palm tree that grows wild. It is harvested when it reaches around 12 feet (4 meters) high. Then it is cut down and sawed in half lengthwise. The pith is scraped out, pounded, boiled on open-air fires, and strained until it is reduced to a pulpy mass. This is then eaten fresh or dried in little pellets to be eaten later. Dried sago, boiled in water, has a sticky, jellylike texture. In cities there are bars serving drinks made from sago, known as bubble tea. Taro is the flesh of corms (underground swollen stems) of lilylike plants. These grow wild in rain forests, but they are also planted in

ball. They then use this to scoop up some sauce or morsels of meat and vegetables. Today in restaurants and Western-style eating places knives and forks are used.

Chicken is the most popular meat in Indonesia, but beef is also a favorite, except in Bali, where the Hindu population does not eat it for religious reasons. Pork is eaten in Christian areas and by Hindus; for Muslims, it is forbidden. Fish and shellfish are plentiful, especially around the coast. In country districts Indonesians also eat unusual meats such as goat, frogs (that live in paddies), dogs, rats, bats, and deer.

Enjoying a tasty snack of rice purchased from a fast-food vendor, this diner uses his right hand to scoop up the rice, Indonesian style.

Gado-Gado

This Indonesian favorite consists of a mixture of vegetables served with a spicy peanut sauce.

You will need:

- 20 oz (600 grams) of your favorite vegetables, washed and cut into bite-sized pieces
- 4 small potatoes, scrubbed, boiled, and left to cool
- 3 hard-boiled eggs
- 2 tsp (10 milliliters) cooking oil
- 1–2 cloves garlic, peeled and chopped
- 1 pinch of chili powder
- 7 oz (200 grams) coconut milk
- 5 oz (140 grams) smooth or crunchy peanut butter
- 2 tsp (10 milliliters) lemon juice
- 2 tsp (10 milliliters) sugar (preferably dark brown)
- 2 tsp (10 milliliters) soy sauce

Steam or microwave the vegetables until tender. Cut the potatoes into thick slices. Shell the hard-boiled eggs and cut them into halves or quarters. Heat the oil in a small pan. Add the garlic and chili powder and cook gently for 2–3 minutes, stirring all the time. Add the coconut milk, peanut butter, lemon juice, sugar, and soy sauce. Stir well. Bring mixture gently to bubbling point, stirring all the time. Add a bit of water if it seems too thick.

Arrange the cooked vegetables, the sliced potatoes, and the hard-boiled eggs on plates, then pour the sauce over. Serve with mango chutney.

This quantity serves four people.

specially cleared fields. When the corms are fully grown they are dug up, cleaned, and then boiled. Cooking makes the flesh very easy to digest.

In Irian Jaya, Papuan sweet potatoes are the traditional local crop. There are over eighty different varieties. All these are boiled and eaten, like rice, with meat, fish, or vegetables, if available. All kinds of vegetables grow well in Indonesia, from worldwide favorites such as tomatoes, squash, and bell peppers to local varieties such as water-spinach, Chinese cabbage, and beans. Indonesians also enjoy products made from soybeans, such as tofu (bean curd) and tempeh (TEHM-peh), a fermented bean cake.

Tempeh—a nutritious cake made from fermented soybeans—displayed at a market in Java. Indonesian cooks use tempeh to make stir-fried dishes or savory pastries.

Whatever its ingredients, most Indonesian food is strongly flavored with chilies; garlic; spices; *terasi* (tuh-RAH-see), a salty shrimp paste; and soy sauce. Ginger, cloves, nutmeg, lemongrass, turmeric, cardamom, and lime leaves are also popular seasonings. Palm sugar (made from tree sap) adds a sweet flavor and sticky texture and is often used in savory dishes as well as in desserts. Coconut and crushed peanuts add richness to many sauces.

Favorite dishes include *nasi goreng* (GOE-ruhng)—rice fried with small pieces of meat and vegetables; *ayam bakar* (IE-uhm BAH-kuhr)—fried chicken; *gado-gado* (GAH-doe GAH-doe)—cooked vegetables with peanut sauce; *babi gulin* (bah-bih-GOO-lihn)—sweet and hot-spiced pork from Bali; *lonton* (LAWN-tawn)—rice steamed in a banana leaf; *rendang* (rehn-DAHNG)—beef and coconut curry; and *satay* (suh-TAE)—small pieces of meat or

Fresh fruit (including lots of bananas), together with many other sweet snacks, on sale at a store on the island of Lombok.

The Durian

Fresh tropical fruits form an important part of the Indonesian diet. Most are sweet and juicy, with a pleasant, tangy taste and a flowery smell. However, one favorite Indonesian fruit—the durian—is famous for combining a delicious flavor with a disgusting odor. Each durian fruit can grow to the size of a small soccer ball. It has a hard, spiky outer skin and creamy white flesh inside. Its flavor is sweet and delicate, but its scent—once opened—can be overpowering. Some people say it smells like blocked drains. For this reason, many airlines and hotels have banned it.

fish grilled on skewers and served with spicy peanut sauce. Many dishes are served with *sambals* (SUHM-buhlz)—mixtures of crushed chilies, spices, and salt.

Indonesian mealtimes are flexible. Many people eat just one main meal a day, in the evening. These evening meals are usually cheerful, social occasions shared by large numbers of family and friends. At other times people eat fruit or buy snacks from street markets and take-out food stalls. Many delicious fruits grow in Indonesia, such as guavas (GWAH-vahz), avocados, mangoes, carambola—a star-shaped tropical fruit, pineapple, snakefruit, bananas, jackfruit, rambutan, soursop, mangosteen—and the incredibly smelly durian (DOOR-yahn). They are eaten fresh, served with crushed ice and sweetened milk or ice cream, or pulped to make healthy, refreshing beverages. Favorite snacks include char-grilled sweetcorn, *murtabak* (MOOR-tah-bahk)—savory pancakes, spring rolls, spicy peanuts, *krupuk* (kruh-PUHK)—fried shrimp crackers, and many kinds of sweet, sticky cakes.

Tea (served very weak, without milk) is the most popular beverage. Indonesia also grows excellent coffee, which is usually served black with lots of sugar, especially at breakfast time. Indonesians like canned and bottled soft beverages, fruit juice, beer, and *arak* (uh-RAHK)—a powerful liquor made from rice or palm sugar. Many Muslim men and women do not drink any alcohol.

After a meal, Indonesian diners traditionally chewed small pellets of *pinang* (peen-ANG) or *betel* (BEH-tuhl). These are made of palm tree nuts, pepper leaves, and powdered lime (a chalky mineral). Betel was believed to freshen the mouth and keep people awake. It also stained the lips and teeth bright red. It was offered to visitors as a sign of welcome; laborers in the fields chewed it to help them keep on working. Today betel is mostly eaten only by older men and women or by people in the countryside.

Arts and Leisure

Indonesia has a rich heritage of arts and crafts. In recent years the Indonesian government and international cultural organizations have worked together to preserve important historic monuments such as the temples at Borobudur, with their wonderful carvings, and the elegant royal palaces in Yogyakarta. Millions of Indonesian vacationers, as well as foreign tourists, now enjoy visiting these sites every year. They also go to see examples of conservation projects that aim to preserve Indonesia's natural heritage, such as the sanctuaries for orangutans on Sumatra and Kalimantan.

Many traditional varieties of music, dancing, and other entertainments are still very popular. The most famous Indonesian music is the gamelan, an orchestra of around thirty gongs and drums, sometimes with a male chorus and women soloists. Gamelans create rippling patterns of sound, unearthly and exciting at the same time. Some people say gamelan music sounds like tropical rain falling. Traditionally performers played at temples to summon people to prayer. They also accompanied performances by puppets and many different kinds of dancers. In the past the oldest gamelan instruments were believed

A Balinese dancer strikes a typically graceful pose. It takes many years of training to learn all the steps, facial expressions, and hand movements of traditional dances.

Instruments of the Gamelan

Each Javanese gamelan orchestra contains many different instruments. Saron and gender are bronze bars on wooden stands; bonang *(boe-NAHNG) and* kenong *(keh-NAWNG) are rows of drum-shaped metal gongs on stands;* kempul *(KEHMP-ool) are hanging bronze gongs, and* gambang *are wooden xylophones, played with sticks of water buffalo horn. There are also* kendang *(drums made of wood and leather),* suling *(bamboo flutes), and* rebab *(two-stringed wooden fiddles played with horsehair bows). There are often two complete sets of instruments in each orchestra, tuned to different scales. Most gamelan performances also include singers and dancers.*

This man plays the gambang (an instrument like a xylophone) in a gamelan orchestra. Many gamelan instruments, like this one, are beautifully decorated with traditional designs.

to be magical. Today there are many gamelan broadcasts on Indonesian radio.

Wayang—large puppets—are an ancient entertainment still very popular today. There are two different kinds. Wayang *kulit* (WIE-uhng KOOLT)—shadow puppets made of leather—perform plays from behind a screen with a light shining behind them. Appearing as giants on the screen, they are operated by men crouching on the floor below them, out of sight in the darkness. Wayang *golek* (GUH-lehk) are made of wood and act on a stage in front of a screen. They are also made to move by hidden operators who are very skillful—and tireless! Performances often last all night long. Both kinds of puppets act out exciting adventure stories from Indian epics—the *Mahabharata* and the *Ramayana*—that are over 2,500 years old.

Gamelan music, dancing, and puppet shows are performed at local festivals, such as *Sekaten* (sae-KAH-tuhn), in Java, which celebrates the prophet Muhammad's birthday, and *Galengun*, on Bali, when ancestor spirits are believed to return to earth. Festival-goers also enjoy watching Pencak Silat—Indonesian martial arts, and in some places, cockfighting, water buffalo races, bullfights, and trials of strength between warriors. Many Indonesian men also like to make bets on all these contests, although this is officially against the law.

All year-round village teams compete in *takrau* (tuh-KROW) matches—a ballgame in which players can use any part of the body, except the hands, to hit the ball around the court. Indonesians also take part in modern sports, especially basketball, volleyball, and badminton. The Indonesian badminton team has been successful in many international competitions and attracts huge crowds. In the late twentieth century Indonesia also became internationally famous as a water sports center. Today tourists visit its beaches to swim and scuba dive for pleasure and relaxation. Surfers from Indonesian islands and many other parts of the world come to ride the huge ocean breakers and to take part in international competitions.

Indonesian people also enjoy many modern entertainments. They watch the latest Hollywood blockbuster movies. Martial arts adventure movies, made in Hong Kong, are also very popular. Young people listen to top international bands and to local stars. Indonesian singers and instrumentalists perform in a number of different styles. *Dangdut* (DAHNG-duht) is fast dance music with a pounding beat, while Pop-Sunda combines love songs based on traditional melodies with

Sekaten

The Sekaten festival, on the island of Java, combines Muslim religious celebrations with older, traditional customs. It honors the birthday of the prophet Muhammad and can last for almost a month. It involves performances of wayang kulit and wayang orang (oe-RANG) — shadow puppet plays, street entertainments, sideshows, and concerts by special Seketan gamelan orchestras. They feature massive, ancient, and extremely loud gongs, kept in the old royal palaces in Surakarta and Yogyakarta. Dating from the first arrival of Islam to Indonesia, the gongs were originally used to summon worshipers to prayers in mosques. Over the centuries people came to think that they had magical powers. The Sekaten festival ends with processions around the old royal palaces and offerings of food to ancient Javanese gods.

A collection of wayang golek puppets from the island of Java. They are skillfully carved from wood and then dressed in silken costumes.

Kerapan Sapi: *Bull Races*

At Madura, in eastern Java, bull races are the most popular entertainment. Pairs of bulls, yoked together, run a 300-foot (100-meter) course, pulling a wooden sled with a driver balanced dangerously behind them. The record time for completing the course is 9 seconds. Top-class bulls are well cared for and are very valuable. Trainers are said to feed their best animals with eggs, honey, and secret mixtures of herbs. Bull races are held all year-round in specially built sports arenas, but the main racing season is September to October, when the championship is held. The championship final is a splendid occasion. Up to one hundred bulls take part, competing in elimination races until just one emerges as the winner. They begin the event with a noisy procession through the streets. The bulls are decorated with ribbons and flowers and accompanied by bands playing flutes, drums, and gongs. The winner of the championship gets a big prize, and spectators bet large sums of money on the result.

electronic instruments, including synthesizers and drums. Popular Nasida Ria is a girl band that sings Qasidah-Modern—Muslim pop songs, often with moral messages. In big cities and tourist areas, especially on Bali, there are many discos and clubs for dancing. People in remote villages listen to music and soap operas on national and local radio stations. If their village has electricity and they can afford the equipment, they might also watch satellite television.

Craftwork

Indonesia is world famous for two special local textiles, batik (buh-TEEK) and ikat (EEK-aht). Batik cloth is richly colored, often with big, bold designs. It is produced by a process called wax resist. The chosen design is "painted" on the cloth with liquid wax. Then the cloth is immersed in vats of dye. The areas not covered by wax absorb the dye. The cloth is then boiled, so that the wax melts and floats away, and the design can be clearly seen against the colored background. This process is repeated several times to create complicated multi-

Trainers get teams of prize bulls—and their drivers—ready to take part in the popular races at Madura, an island off the northeast coast of Java.

Each length of thread used to make ikat cloth is dyed before it is woven. This means that the weavers have to work out the pattern in advance—an enormously difficult task.

including formal suits for businesspeople and jeans and T-shirts for laborers and vacationers. For wealthy customers, Indonesian designers create fantastic fashions, inspired by the latest looks from Paris and Milan as well as traditional clothing styles.

Each region of Indonesia has its own local crafts, such as pottery and basketmaking on Lombok. Indonesians make use of local materials, such as clay or fibers from tropical plants, and their work often reflects each region's history. For example, delicate gold and silver jewelry made on Bali is influenced by ancient Hindu designs. There is also a modern tradition of painting on Bali. This began in the early twentieth century, when European artists who settled there taught local people how to paint pictures in a Western style.

Skilled iron craftspeople live on many Indonesian islands. On Java they make kris (KREES)—daggers with curved blades and decorated handles that were traditionally believed to have magical powers. These powers came from all the people—usually ancestors—who had once used the kris. In the past, fathers handed over the family kris to their teenage sons as a sign that they had become adults, and today they are still prized possessions. In Kalimantan, craftspeople use iron to make sacred *parang* blades, used for farming and fighting. They, too, are believed to have magic powers.

Fine wood and stone carving is found throughout Indonesia, but today craftspeople often use traditional skills originally developed to decorate houses, temples, and other ceremonial buildings to create items for the tourist trade.

colored patterns. Often, the dye seeps underneath the wax in places to create an attractive marbled effect. Ikat cloth is also brightly patterned, but the designs are created by carefully dyeing the threads before they are woven. This takes great skill and experience. Weaving ikat cloth is also an expert process. The finest pieces of fabric can take over a month to finish.

Batik and ikat are used to make traditional scarves and sarongs worn by men and women in villages and also to make shirts, skirts, shorts, and dresses. In cities and tourist areas of Indonesia, most people like to wear Western-style clothes,

Glossary

adat customs and traditions, unwritten laws.

agribusiness the businesses and operations that are associated with farming.

aid agency an association that provides people with help in times of need, such as water and food during drought.

alliance a group of two or more people, organizations, or countries working together with the same aims.

animism the belief that things in nature, such as trees, mountains, and the sky, have souls or consciousness.

archaeology the scientific study of ancient cultures through the examination of their material remains, such as fossil relics, monuments, and tools.

archipelago a group or chain of islands; a wide stretch of water with many scattered islands.

atheism the belief that there is no God.

bankrupt a state of being unable to pay off debts.

civil service the administrative service of a government that takes care of the business of running a state but does not include the lawmaking branch, the military, or the court system.

colony a country or area that is ruled by another country.

communist a believer in communism, a theory that suggests that all property belongs to the community and that work should be organized for the common good.

coral reef a marine reef composed of the skeletons of tiny organisms called polyps, together with minerals and organic matter.

coup a brilliant, sudden, and usually highly successful act, particularly the violent overthrow of an existing government by a small group.

democracy a state ruled by the people; a state in which government is carried out by representatives elected by the public.

dialect a nonstandard version of a language, such as one spoken in a particular region or by a particular group of people.

dynasty a ruling family.

enterprise a new, often risky, business project that involves confidence and initiative.

epic a long story of heroic events and actions.

famine a severe shortage of food, usually resulting in widespread hunger.

fundamentalism a movement supporting strict and literal observance of guidelines, particularly religious ones, that often involves taking extreme social or political positions.

heritage the traditions, status, and character acquired by being born into a particular family or social class.

human rights rights that are considered by society to belong automatically to everyone.

inflation an overall increase in the price of goods and services in a country.

irrigate to supply land with water brought through pipes or ditches.

mangrove any of various tropical trees or shrubs that grow roots and form dense masses in salty marshes or shallow saltwater.

Middle East the countries of southwest Asia and northeast Africa — usually thought to include the countries extending from Libya in the west to Afghanistan in the east.

migrant somebody who moves from one place to another in search of work or economic opportunities.

monk a member of a religious community made up of men who devote themselves to prayer, solitude, and contemplation.

monopoly complete control over the entire supply of goods or a service in a certain market.

nationalism a loyalty or devotion to a country; the promotion of policies designed to benefit and support a particular nation.

natural resource a natural material, such as coal or wood, that can be exploited by people.

nomadic describes people who do not have a permanent home but instead move from place to place, usually in search of pasture for their animals.

peninsula a piece of land sticking out from the mainland into a sea or lake.

poverty line a level of income below which someone is considered poor.

province a division of a country having its own government.

rattan a climbing palm with long, tough stems.

rebellion opposition to authority; an attempt to overthrow a government using violence.

revolution an attempt by a large group of people to change their country's political system, often using force.

sarong a long strip of cloth wrapped loosely around the body and worn by men and women.

separatist a person who favors separation from a religious group, country, or an organization or group of any sort.

shaman somebody who acts as a go-between for the physical and spiritual realms and who is said to have particular powers such as healing.

slash-and-burn a form of agriculture where trees and vegetation are cut down and burned in order to plant crops in their place.

treaty an agreement or contract between two or more states or rulers.

tsunami a great sea wave produced by a volcano eruption or earthquake under the sea.

United Nations an alliance, founded in 1945, that today includes most of the countries in the world. Its aim is to encourage international cooperation and peace.

Further Reading

Internet Sites
Look under Countries A to Z in the Atlapedia Online Web Site at
     http://www.atlapedia.com
Use the drop-down menu to select a country on the CIA World Factbook Web Site at
     http://www.odci.gov/cia/publications/factbook
Browse the Table of Contents in the Library of Congress Country Studies Web Site at
     http://lcweb2.loc.gov/frd/cs/cshome.html
Use the Country Locator Maps in the World Atlas Web Site at
     http://www.worldatlas.com/aatlas/world.htm
Look under the alphabetical country listing using the Infoplease Atlas at
     http://www.infoplease.com/countries.html
Use the drop-down menu to select a country using E-Conflict™ World Encyclopedia at
     http://www.emulateme.com
Look under the alphabetical country listing in the Yahooligans Around the World Directory at
     http://www.yahooligans.com/Around_the_World/Countries
Choose the part of the world you're interested in, then scroll down to choose the country using the Geographia Web Site at
     http://www.geographia.com

Indonesia
Costain, Meredith, and Paul Collins. *Welcome to Indonesia (Countries of the World)*. Philadelphia, PA: Chelsea House Publishers, 2001.

Cramer, Mark, and Frederick Fisher. *Indonesia (Countries of the World)*. Milwaukee, WI: Gareth Stevens, 2000

Daley, Patrick. *Indonesia (Steadwell Books World Tour)*. Austin, TX: Raintree Steck-Vaughn, 2002

Gerst, Tom. *Indonesia in Pictures*. Minneapolis, MN: Lerner Publications Company, 1995.

Lyle, Gary. *Indonesia (Major World Nations)*. Philadelphia, PA: Chelsea House Publishers, 1998.

Mesenas, Geraldine, and Frederick Fisher. *Welcome to Indonesia (Welcome to My Country)*. Milwaukee, WI: Gareth Stevens, 2001

Mirpuri, Gouri. *Indonesia (Cultures of the World)*. Tarrytown, NY: Marshall Cavendish, 1994.

Riehecky, Janet. *Indonesia (Countries of the World)*. Mankato, MN.: Bridgestone, 2002.

Simpson, Judith. *Indonesia (Ask about Asia)*. Philadelphia, PA: Mason Crest Publishers, 2002.

Index

Page numbers in *italic* indicate illustrations.

Page numbers in *italic* indicate illustrations.